Basildon, Our Heritage

Basildon, Our Heritage

Frances Clamp

Photographs & Photographic Advice
Bob Fisher

The History Press

First published 2008
Reprinted 2019

The History Press Ltd
97 St George's Place, Cheltenham,
Gloucestershire, GL50 3QB
www.thehistorypress.co.uk

British Library Cataloguing in Publication Data.
A catalogue record for this book is available from the British Library.

ISBN 978 0 7524 4551 9

Typesetting and origination by The History Press Ltd.
Printed in Great Britain by TJ International Ltd, Padstow, Cornwall.

Contents

Foreword

Over forty years later I can still remember my first sight of Basildon.

My dad's factory was leaving London to relocate here, and before we moved he had been commuting daily in the back of a van. I remember viewing our new corporation house in Pitsea. Looking around Basildon, I loved the green spaces and all the trees. But the sight that really caught my eye was the huge, largely glass structure on the edge of Gloucester Park – the swimming pool. As a regular swimmer I was used to Hackney Baths and I was thrilled that this would be 'my' pool.

We loved our new home. Mum and Dad still live there and all the things we now take for granted – inside loo, a bathroom and central heating – were a first for us. I had my own bedroom, which I made Dad paint purple. (When I left home it took him years to cover up my youthful attempt at interior design!)

I then attended Pitsea and Chalvedon schools (later becoming a governor), worked at Rita Smith's store in Pitsea market, swam for Basildon Swimming Club, attended the Towngate for pottery on Saturday mornings and very soon called Basildon 'home'.

It has been my honour to have been the county councillor for Pitsea and now a Member of Parliament for my home town. I'm the first really 'local' MP and I often tell the kids I meet in schools that when I go I hope it's someone local that takes over – we can produce our own Member of Parliament. It is an honour and a privilege.

Basildon has given me tremendous opportunities in life and I really appreciate that. It's not a perfect town – where is? But it's my town. My home.

Angela Smith
January 2008

Dedication

This book is dedicated to the young people of Basildon on whom the future of the New Town depends, and to those early pioneers who had to work so hard, often through extremely arduous circumstances, so that they might leave a more optimistic legacy to future generations of Basildonians.

Vin Harrop
January 2008

Acknowledgements

I would like to thank all those who have helped with the writing of this book.

Very special mention must be made of David Fisher, without whose help it would have remained a dream, Bob Fisher for the many hours he has spent taking and arranging photographs, Vin Harrop who thought of the idea of a Heritage Trail and all the members of the Heritage Project team including Elizabeth Grant and Lisa Horner. Thanks must also go to the headteachers, staff and children of the five schools involved, to Ken Porter, the rector, the Rev. Esther McCafferty and members of St Martin of Tours, Basildon PCC, Hans Wusterfeld, Kim Stafford, Joan Merrison, Gary Houghton and Adam Keating, members of Brentwood Writers' Circle, Sylvia Kent and to all those who have contributed in any way to make this book a success.

Above all I must thank Roger, my husband, who has helped in so many ways.

Bob Fisher's email address: bob_fisher@btopenworld.com

Every effort has been made to trace ownership of photographs and to check that the facts given in this book are correct. My apologies for any unwitting errors or omissions.

Frances Clamp,
June 2008

The Basildon Heritage Trail and Basildon Heritage Project have been supported by Basildon Council, Essex County Council, The Heritage Lottery and Veolia ES Cleanaway Pitsea Marshes Trust.

1

Looking Back

Long Ago

The term *Basildon New Town* suggests that nothing existed before the creation of the new development. Of course this is completely wrong. Traces of life dating from at least 3,000 BC have been found in the Downham area and a Neolithic stone hammerhead was discovered when the roundabout at the junction of Whitmore Way and Timberlog Lane was under construction.

As time passed other settlers moved into the area. Evidence of flint-tool making has been found at Langdon Hills and Late Bronze Age implements were uncovered during the building of Swan Mead, now Cherry Tree Primary School. (See Chapter 5)

We know that Iron Age settlements also existed in various parts of the Basildon area. Whether the Romans came here is unknown, although some bricks and tiles, dating from the time of their occupation, have been found in Vange.

Times of Change

Basildon, Laindon, Pitsea and Vange are all names that have Saxon origins. Basildon was originally known as Beorhtel's Hill. The Saxons preferred to settle away from major Roman settlements and this is the time when many small villages grew up.

With the arrival of the Normans, life changed forever for the inhabitants of England. In the Domesday Book, compiled from 1086, Basildon appears as part of the Barnstable Hundred. In the following centuries the name is occasionally mentioned in records, but it appears to have been an area of small villages and manors devoted to farming. There was an annual fair held at Basildon from the Middle Ages and this continued until around 1848, but the original charter no longer exists. It is believed the site of this fair may have been where Fairhouse Farm once stood and later the site was developed as Fairhouse School.

Outside Cherry Tree School where Late Bronze Age artifacts were found during the construction.
(© Bob Fisher)

The Middle Ages and Beyond

In 1388 The Black Death struck families and villages throughout the whole country and Essex too experienced a considerable reduction in its population. This led to discontent among the peasants and a number of men from the county are known to have joined the ill-fated Peasants' Revolt. The change from arable to sheep farming caused further population decline. Later both men and women from the area, especially from Billericay, are known to have sailed to America with the first settlers. However, for much of the time until the late nineteenth century farming continued to be the main occupation, with small manors and farms continuing to thrive.

The Coming of the Railway

Farming was never easy in Essex. Much of the soil is heavy clay and towards the coast marshy land brought its own problems. Yet the farmers continued to make a living until two things happened to dramatically change their lives and the use of their land.

Firstly, in 1882 an Act of Parliament allowed the London, Tilbury & Southend Railway Company (LTSRC) to construct a direct line from London to Southend. The work was finally completed in 1889 and included two new stations, one at Laindon and another at Pitsea. In 1871 the passing of the Bank Holiday Act had allowed more freedom of travel. Many Londoners from the east and north discovered the joys of leaving the city for a day to spend their time by the seaside. Some preferred to explore the countryside en route and both the new stations became well used, especially at weekends. Cheap fares encouraged even more travellers to venture away from their usual haunts.

This was not enough for the railway companies. They wanted passengers using their trains every day throughout the year. If property speculators acquired land along the rail routes then more people would be encouraged to move away from London and they would then use the trains to travel in to work. If the railway companies and the land agents worked together then the results could be extremely profitable for both.

Farm Failures

The second dramatic change happened in farming itself. Ever since the late 1870s agricultural land, especially in south-east Essex, had been falling into disuse. The soil around Basildon was heavy clay. It retained water when it rained but became rock hard and cracked in hot weather. This was particularly bad in the late 1870s and early 1880s. At the same time cheap wheat started arriving from America, flooding the British markets. This suited the railway companies and the developers. More farmland went out of use. Farming in the area started collapsing and the eager land agents were ready to benefit.

Here we see an early photograph of Laindon Station Post Office. (Gary Houghton's archives)

The Coming of the Land Agents

Faced with bankruptcy or accepting low payment for their land meant that many farmers were only too willing to sell up and move into other employment. The agents soon realised that the best way to recoup their investment quickly was to divide the land into small plots and sell these at low prices to Londoners, still leaving themselves with a good profit. Possibly the largest of these agents was the Land Co. of London. Once the land was acquired, plans could be drawn up showing the plots and offering them for sale. Many single plots were just 18ft wide but length varied according to position.

Advertisements were placed in newspapers and at railway stations in London as the agents looked for purchasers. Cheap fares were offered to take prospective purchasers to auctions held on the estates. These were usually between April to October, when the countryside was at its most inviting, but finishing before the start of really bad weather. Sometimes there were free lunches and even champagne to attract people to the sales. New buyers used the railway to reach the sites, so both the land agents and the railway companies benefited from the sales. The land furthest from the stations was cheaper than that close by. Some buyers put down deposits, but so enjoyed the liquid hospitality offered that they completely forgot about their purchases afterwards. This was to cause huge problems later when the New Town was ready for development. Tracing some plot holders became a nightmare.

Three plotland cottages in Pound Lane, Pitsea. (Gary Houghton's archives)

New Arrivals

The Basildon area was advertised as being extremely healthy. The fact that Pitsea was without a doctor was even used as a selling point. Prospective buyers were informed that this showed what an excellent environment the village was to settle in!

Many of the early plotlanders had little money to spare. When they made their weekend trips to their very own piece of land in the country the first thing needed was shelter, both for themselves and for their tools. Bell tents were often used before more substantial sheds could be erected. These were sometimes rented out to friends who also wanted to enjoy the delights of a day in the country.

Hardships

Although some still remember life on the plotlands with nostalgia, in many respects the dwellings were far from idyllic. Many lacked gas, electricity, water and drainage. If you were simply camping for a weekend then these hardships could be part of the fun, but by the 1920s and 1930s many more buyers arrived, ready to acquire their very own piece of country life. In some cases permanent dwellings were built, often of wood but others were of brick. Many of these grew from the original sheds, but they were still without amenities.

Getting Established

Albert Lee, who still lives in Basildon, remembers the day his father came home to announce that he had bought a plot of land. It was quite large, being of around five acres and thickly covered in brambles. He acquired an old ship's cabin and this became the centrepiece of the bungalow that was later built on the site.

At first some people stayed in former railway carriages, old buses or just wooden sheds. There may have been hardships, but all seem to have loved their trips away from the smoke of the East End.

Growing Up on the Laindon Plotlands

Sheila Nichols, nee Pigram, well remembers growing up in 'Eleanor', a dwelling built by her father. Although he was not a builder, Sheila lived in the brick-built home he constructed from the time she was a baby until she left to marry at the age of twenty. The house had a frontage of approximately 60ft, the width of three plots, and also had a very long garden. This was in Markhams Chase, a made-up road. Such plots were far more expensive than those on unmade tracks.

Growing up was a real adventure in this rural area. However, when the war came, Laindon received many young evacuees, sent to stay with relatives in the comparative safety of the countryside. These were private arrangements, but the young Londoners brought with them more sophisticated expectations than those previously enjoyed by Sheila and her friends.

The Laindon Hotel. (Gary Houghton's archives)

They were used to Saturday-morning cinema visits and the young Laindoners wanted similar entertainment.

The local school was Markhams Chase Primary where the headmistress was the charismatic Janet Duke. It was a large school for those days with around 400 pupils. It was later split into a separate junior and infant school. The junior school has since been renamed and is now The Janet Duke Memorial School after the headmistress who made such a profound impression on her young charges.

Problems

For many there was the problem of the long walk from the station. This was often along unmade roads thick with clay. Sturdy boots were essential and old prams and hand-made carts were frequently used to transport building materials and other possessions to the plots. These small hardships were accepted cheerfully by most of the new settlers. They were only too thankful to be away from their ordinary London life.

The Depression struck in the 1920s with the General Strike following in 1926. Less money was available and many who had intended developing their plots with more permanent buildings now found this impossible. As a result some sites were left for months or even years before the money was found to build habitable properties. Other plots were simply abandoned.

Services

When nine-year-olds in 2007 were asked what they would have missed most if they had been plotlanders, the majority decided that the answer was gas. This caused some surprise amongst the adults, but the reason given was that it would be impossible to keep the homes warm! These are children who have grown up in a time of central heating.

For the early settlers one of the first things they needed to do was arrange toilet facilities. Sometimes this was a wooden-earth closet, or simply a screened bucket with a large trench where the contents could be emptied and earth shovelled over the top. Later, wooden huts were often built, well away from the dwelling. The bedroom in the Plotlands Museum at Laindon has a chamber pot under the bed, a reminder that night-time visits to the outside toilet would have been extremely unpleasant, especially in bad weather.

A lockable shed was also a priority as tools and garden implements needed to be stored safely, even before building commenced.

Murder!

Water often came from a communal tap and children enjoyed being sent with buckets and jugs to collect the precious liquid. However, it was a water shortage that led to a notorious murder.

The year was 1906. Albert Watson and his wife Emma lived in a small shack in Honeypot Lane. In their garden was a pond from which they obtained their water. Unfortunately very little rain fell that year and the pond dried up. The couple decided to take water from a pond at nearby Sawyer's Farm. Two brothers from the farm, Richard and Robert Buckham, aged twenty and seventeen, objected and one of them shot the couple six times at close range. Richard later confessed to the killing and was hanged in December, three months after the murder. His younger brother was acquitted.

Weekends Away

At first many of the plotlanders used their small shacks as weekend retreats. There are still many stories told of those who spent childhood weekends in summer away from London, travelling instead to the rural surroundings of Essex. There were trees to be climbed and adventures to be enjoyed in the country setting while their parents grew flowers and vegetables in the gardens. On Sunday evenings the families would return to the crowded stations at Laindon and Pitsea, laden down with their garden produce and ready to travel back to the city.

When the plotlands flourished in the 1920s and 1930s local traders really benefited from the influx of customers at weekends and holiday times. Carey's in Laindon High Road supplied building materials and made sure that anything ordered one week was delivered the next so that work could start as soon as the plot holders arrived.

Needless to say, the actual construction of the buildings was a challenge. Tools and essential materials had to be carried from the station and new skills were needed to make safe dwellings. Yet gradually the work was completed and a spirit of friendship grew between those living on the estates. Homeowners would always look out for the needs of their neighbours.

There is no definite date for this photograph of a charabanc and motorcycle outside the Fortune of War, Laindon, although the motorcycle was first registered in 1920. The reason for the fancy dress in also unknown, but may well have been associated with a carnival. (Gary Houghton's archives)

It is well worth reading *Basildon Plotlands* by Deanna Walker (details in the Bibliography) to get a feel of the life of a child growing up when the plotlands were flourishing in Laindon.

War!

The London Blitz made life for anyone living in the East End, and especially those close to the docks, unbearable. As bombs fell night after night those with plots in Basildon realised that they had a way to escape. Surely it would be safer living in the country. Many made their plans and moved.

Unfortunately this dream was short lived. German bombers often followed the River Thames or the Southend Arterial Road (A127), using them as guides when flying to and from the capital. This led to the skies over Basildon becoming extremely dangerous as bombs were dropped on buildings below to lighten loads as pilots attempted to escape from British fighter planes. Around Essex there were many anti-aircraft gun emplacements and it was not uncommon for searchlights to criss-cross the night sky, endeavouring to pick up the escaping German planes. Some were shot down, causing devastation below.

Laindon High Street in the early years of the twentieth century. (Gary Houghton's archives)

Casualties

By the end of the war twenty-four people had been killed in the area, with ninety- two seriously injured and a further 454 receiving minor injuries. 149 homes were completely demolished and 6,100 damaged. This was not such a safe haven after all! Most of the bombs dropped were not aimed at specific targets, although the railways and major roads might well have been the objective of some planes.

Gardeners Lane has its own unique place in Basildon's war history. The first bombs to fall landed there in August 1940, damaging four cottages. This was also one of the last roads to be hit, this time by a V2 rocket in March 1945.

Situated close to Rectory Road, on a site later partly occupied by the Ford tractor plant, stood the Basildon Rectory. This was a particularly unfortunate building. It was badly damaged by two bombs in September 1940. Then, in January 1945, a V2 rocket hit the same building and in March of the same year another V2 landed in almost the same spot.

Children swimming in Pitsea Creek, possibly in the 1930s. (Gary Houghton's archives)

New Beginnings

As the war finally ended some must have hoped that Basildon would return once more to the type of area it had been before those dark days. However, war had changed too many things for such dreams to ever be fulfilled.

There were many miles of unmade roads and tiny houses still without proper facilities. Although the pride of their owners, these had often been built in a sub-standard way. The population had also increased dramatically during the war years and just afterwards, reaching 20,000, a threefold increase since the days before the war. Many families who had settled in Basildon, Laindon and Pitsea during those troubled times were unwilling to return to the devastation that remained around their old homes and often soldiers coming home after demob preferred to settle in the countryside.

For Billericay Urban District Council this was a nightmare. Roads had to be improved and the state of housing brought up to modern standards. Many of the small dwellings had a rateable value of less than £10. The cost of improvements to the plotlanders' houses would be prohibitive. A sudden increase in rates would mean that some would be unable to continue living in their properties. Yet where would they go? Thousands of homes in the east of London had been destroyed and it would take years before they could be rebuilt. There seemed no answer to the problems.

New Towns

Then, in 1944, even before the end of the war, Sir Patrick Abercrombie and his team suggested that new towns should be created within greenbelt areas. They would be well designed, with industry being encouraged within the plans. The new inhabitants would be able to find local work and thus avoid the stress of daily long-distance travel. This was known as the Greater London Plan. In 1946 the New Towns Act was passed and it was decided that there would be five New Towns in the Home Counties. Essex was seen as suitable for two of these towns. Margaretting, Ongar and Harlow were considered, but the first two rejected. At that point Basildon was not included in the recommendations.

This was the ideal opportunity for Billericay Urban District Council. If they were accepted as a New Town their financial problems would be over. The Council Clerk, Mr Alma Hatt, worked tirelessly to try to have Basildon accepted as one of the New Towns. By October 1946 he was ready to send an official letter to the Minister of Town and Country Planning laying out the case for the town. He was actively supported by the boroughs of East and West Ham, both of which had a desperate shortage of housing following the war. Many of those already living in Basildon had come from east London so it seemed an excellent solution to expand this area. By May 1948 provisional approval was given by the government.

The Start of Basildon New Town

It took time before residents fully realised what was about to happen. Then householders became aware that their freehold ownership was likely to be threatened. Protests started, especially in Laindon. Sheila Nichols recalls the lack of enthusiasm shown by many of the plotlanders to the plans. Most people were not offered enough money to buy alternative homes, just enough to purchase some new furniture when they moved into rented accommodation. Many were very proud of being owner occupiers and to have to leave their own homes was certainly a retrograde step. Sheila's father stood out for more money, but by the time a Compulsory Purchase Order was issued on their home the bungalow was surrounded by a sea of mud, as most of the other houses had already been demolished.

A Time of Change

Yet, by the time the Minister of Town and Country Planning attended a meeting in Laindon in October 1948, plans for the New Town were already far advanced. By the following January, Basildon's New Town status was confirmed.

The designation document stated that Basildon Development Corporation would bear most of the development costs and this included purchase of land and buildings, road construction, drainage and the building of houses, shops and the smaller industrial units. The area involved consisted of 7,818 acres. It was difficult land with a railway cutting across the middle and there were 30,000 different ownerships in the area, many of them unknown and almost impossible to trace.

Pitsea shops and the Broadway cinema. (Gary Houghton's archives)

A target figure of a population of 50,000 was originally set for the New Town. Many felt that this was unrealistic. By that time there was already a population of 25,000. Some felt that 80,000 would be a more realistic aim. There was the belief that the town would be a self-supporting, self-contained community, although it was realised that many of the original inhabitants would continue to travel to work away from the area.

Over the years there have been many changes to details in the master plan. One thing that has caused problems has been the growth of car ownership. Few garages and parking spaces were catered for in the original plan. Adaptations have been made over the years to cope with the great changes in transport during this time.

New Arrivals

A real Red Letter Day for Basildon came on 18 June 1951. That was when the first of the tenants moved into the newly built houses. Betty and John Walker were the very first couple to receive their keys to a house in Redgrave Road in Vange. Others quickly followed. The New Town was on its way.

Of course, not everyone was happy. Many of the old plotholders hated the changes that were being made. Yet compulsory purchase orders soon meant that they had little choice but to accept their new situation.

For those early tenants life was far from easy. At first they lived in the middle of a building site and although some small shops did exist, they were far from ideal for the newcomers. However, mobile traders soon saw the advantages of delivering goods to the new developments. Needless to say, they were welcomed by the new householders.

Work and Housing

In 1957 Maire Pedder obtained a job at Bonnalack's, a firm building bodies for lorries. At first she travelled to Basildon daily from Dagenham, but within three weeks of starting work she was offered a new two-bedroomed corporation house in The Hatherly. Marley flooring had been used in the ground-floor rooms. At that time her husband, Peter, was still completing his National Service in Germany.

Little of the town centre had been built at that time and the majority of shoppers appeared to be pushing prams. In fact this area became known locally as 'Nappy Valley'.

On his return from Germany, Peter worked in the booking offices at Laindon and Pitsea railway stations and Maire moved to another well-known company, Marconi.

Inside Pitsea Congregational Church. (Gary Houghton's archives)

A Fresh Start

It was in 1964 that Pat and Laurie Woollard moved from Lincolnshire into a brand-new house in Basildon. At that time there was a shortage of teachers in New Towns and those newly appointed were also offered housing by the corporation. Pat applied for a job at Laindon School. She was immediately offered a post as Head of Home Economics. At that time the family was still without accommodation and places were also needed in a nursery school for their two young sons. The headmaster suggested that she should visit the corporation office, which she did. He had obviously started phoning as soon as she left his office as she was promptly offered a new house with three bedrooms. Nursery places were also found for the children on the same day.

Pat remembers how delighted they were to find that the house had under-floor central heating. Unfortunately this was extremely expensive to run, so use had to be kept to a minimum. Most of the neighbours had come from Dagenham to work in the Ford factory. Visits to the town centre are also recalled. At that time it all appeared to be very clean and new, although there were still many spaces awaiting future development.

Gradually, things improved for the newcomers. Shops were opened, community centres built and new churches served the spiritual needs of the community. Of course, schools were also necessary and old ones were extended with new ones coming into being, ready for an ever-expanding population of youngsters.

The bus station overlooked by the mosaic depicting the history of Basildon, *c.* 1960. (Gary Houghton's archives)

Goodbye to the Plotlanders

Not everyone was happy. Some of the plotlanders moved into the new accommodation and were delighted with the services available. Yet for many a way of life they loved was being destroyed before their eyes. The green countryside that had drawn them like magnets over the years was now rapidly disappearing under a sea of concrete. Compulsory purchase meant, for many, the end of a dream. Some were losing their weekend retreats, but for many it was the homes they had built and loved that were now being taken away and destroyed. Times were changing. There was no doubt that the plotlands could not have survived as they were, but that didn't stop those who wanted to preserve their way of life from fighting until further protest became impossible.

The Plotlands Museum

In Third Avenue, Laindon, off Lower Dunton Road, it is still possible to visit one small bungalow, now preserved as a museum. This is The Haven. It stands on land controlled by the Essex Wildlife Trust and is an excellent place to visit. You will find extremely helpful and knowledgeable volunteers in the visitors centre and there is good parking if you choose to stroll between the remains of some of the ruined cottages until you reach The Haven.

The Market, *c.* 1965. (Gary Houghton's archives)

Although the museum is not open all the time, it is well worth trying to go when it is. This was one of the more substantial dwellings and covered three plots, each one costing £9 in the early 1930s. It has been preserved with furniture and equipment from the 1930s and there is even an Anderson shelter in the garden.

The Haven was in the hands of the Mills family for two generations, the plot measuring 60ft x 120ft. There were very few planning regulations in those days, so each new home represented the individuality of its owners.

The New Town Grows

In 1801, according to the census, Basildon had a population of just sixty-two. In Laindon there were 304 and in Pitsea 211. The 2001 census recorded 165,668 inhabitants in the whole Basildon area. The number now will have increased even more.

During the construction of the New Town many fascinating architectural features were included. In fact, this must have been an architect's dream project. Over the years some of these features have been ignored or allowed to fall into disrepair. The new Heritage Trail – Chapters 3 and 4 – will visit many of these gems from the past and we can only hope that a journey around the route will give the Basildonians of today a new awareness of the town and all it has to offer.

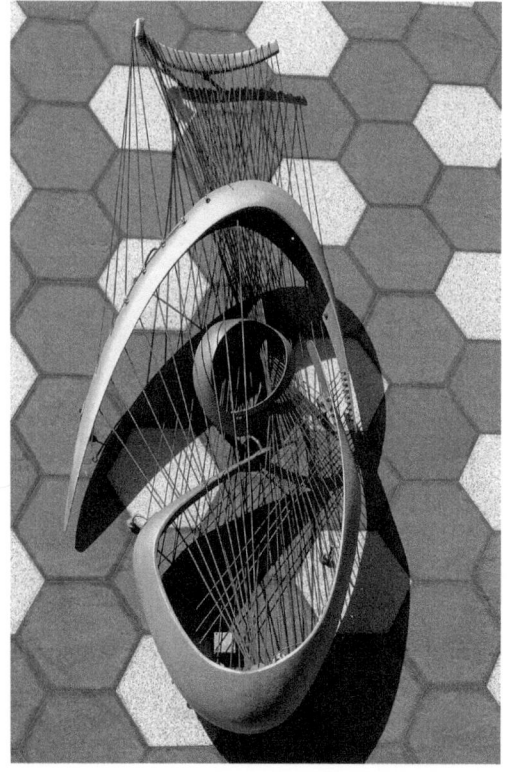

The Treble Clef on Freedom House.

2

The Basildon Heritage Project

A Friend of Basildon

The Basildon Heritage Project was the brainchild of Vin Harrop. He started his connection with Basildon in 1967. That was when he arrived to run the first purpose-built local authority Arts Centre in the country, located in a temporary building designed to last for seven years. In fact it was finally demolished fourteen years later, a move deeply regretted by those who had enjoyed the facilities.

The Arts Centre stood where the Westgate Shopping Centre is now, alongside the Towngate Theatre building. In those days there was provision for a theatre and cinema, with separate areas for pottery, sculpture and photography. The designer of the Arts Centre, Ken Cotton, was also responsible for the swimming pool in Gloucester Park.

After three years Vin resigned, but his interest in the local arts scene continued. In 1979 he helped with the establishment of The Fold Arts Centre in Billericay and in 1999 he founded the commission for an Essex Arts Gallery. This was with other like-minded people, all of whom dreamed of having a space for indigenous art in Essex. They felt the need for a home where all the arts could be displayed, something that had not formerly existed in the county. In April 2006 the name was changed to the Foundation for Essex Arts.

At the same time there were discussions with CABE, the Commission for Architecture and Built Environment, with thoughts of establishing an Essex architectural centre. New houses were being built in the county and it was felt that a group was needed to lobby for quality design. This is something that is frequently ignored in the rush to build new properties as quickly as possible. The group would help local councillors to gain the strength and knowledge to champion design when discussing new developments. CABE agreed to pay for a feasibility study. Approximately nine months were needed to complete the work and it was finally agreed that Essex should have a centre for architecture. Vin Harrop's group became this centre, but a building was still desperately needed.

When the early pioneers arrived in the New Town of Basildon they found very few amenities. The original plan was for self-sufficient neighbourhoods, each with its own doctor, dentist, community centre, grocer and all the other needs of people who had moved from their former tight-knit communities. Unfortunately, that was not how things worked out. Shoppers needed to visit the town centre for their requirements, but even getting there was difficult for those in

Vin Harrop. (© Bob Fisher)

Outside the Towngate Theatre and the Basildon Centre. (© Bob Fisher)

Pupils from St Anne Line School taking photographs with their teacher, Paul Davis. (© Bob Fisher)

the outlying areas as the bus service was still poor and the number of shops limited. Once the Arts Centre was open it did give a cultural focus.

The Basildon Heritage Project

The members of the Architecture Centre of Essex (ACE) felt that it would be an excellent idea to create a project where the young people of Basildon could be made aware of the town's built environment, its architecture and wide, open spaces. These ideas had been carefully incorporated in the original plans for the town. From this initial birth came The Basildon Heritage Project.

The aim was to make the children of Basildon more aware of their environment and to understand about the place where they live. Many of the early settlers in the New Town were uprooted from London and they lacked a sense of history in their new environment. If children understand the past they are likely to pass on this knowledge to future generations.

A decision was taken to approach all the primary schools in the town to see if any wished to be involved in the pilot scheme. Most liked the idea but finally five expressed a firm interest and decided to take part. These were Bardfield Primary School, Cherry Tree Primary School, Laindon Park Primary School, Pitsea Junior School and St Ann Line Roman Catholic School. Together with these schools it was decided that a Heritage Trail was needed in Basildon to show

Our town, our heritage

The Basildon Heritage Project Team: *Back row:* Vin Harrop, Bob Fisher. *Front row:* Frances Clamp, Lisa Horner, Elizabeth Grant.

all residents and visitors points of particular interest and importance in the town. The children would participate in making this happen. To cover the cost of creating this trail an application was made to The Heritage Lottery Fund. This is a long and sometimes difficult process and much work was involved before the application could be submitted. The children would also be involved in creating and following a pilot route.

The Team

It was soon apparent that a team would be needed to visit schools and talk to the children. Then came the idea that if they were to learn more about their own history, environment and local architecture, they might see things more clearly through the eye of a camera. Grants were applied for and Essex County Council and Basildon Council were willing to support the proposal.

Vin Harrop then began searching for a suitable photographer. A number of people showed interest but, for various reasons, they proved to be unsuitable. Then Bob Fisher arrived on the scene. He had been involved in education throughout his working life and was a very keen and knowledgeable photographer. He also had that essential quality needed for a project of this type – boundless enthusiasm! His love of photography started during his own schooldays when he became president of the school photographic society in the 1950s.

It was decided that enough digital cameras must be bought to ensure that all the children involved had the chance to get hands-on experience of using this type of equipment. Canon A540 digital compact cameras were chosen as being the most suitable for the project. Bob's own photographs are often taken on a Sony DSC-R1 Cybershot 10.3 Megapixel camera and he prints on glossy or satin paper using an Epson 2100 printer.

Twenty-two cameras were finally purchased and Bob went into the schools to work with small groups from Year 5. Most of the children were in the nine-to-ten age group. This was in the autumn term of 2006. The children soon caught his enthusiasm and surprisingly quickly began to learn new skills. At first they borrowed the cameras for a week at a time and went around their own schools and the surrounding area putting what they had learned into practice. The results were impressive.

The Team Expands

A writer was also needed. The photographs required written explanations showing why a certain shot had been chosen and what special details could be seen. It was also decided to include some creative writing, using facts about the history of the town and weaving them into fictional stories. That is where my own involvement with the project started. As a former teacher and

Frances Clamp helped children with their writing.

On the trail in Gloucester Park with pupils from Cherry Tree School. (© Bob Fisher)

writer of fiction books for children and also seven local history books I, too, felt that I might have something to contribute.

Elizabeth Grant joined the team to give her help and support to the project. She had been involved with the Commission for an Essex Gallery since 1999 and is a trustee of the Essex Arts Group. Among other things she brought in a film unit from Woodlands School and members of this team joined the children on several occasions.

Lisa Horner, a keen local artist, is a member of START (Support Through Art), a group of Basildon-based artists who work with children and adults as they strive to express themselves through art. They are behind the very successful 'Studio 2' and the South Essex Open Exhibition. These originally started at Bardfield School but later moved to Barleylands. When she offered her services as a researcher she quickly became an invaluable part of the Heritage Project. The team was complete.

Into the Schools

Visits were made to all the schools. The children heard about the early plotlanders and then wrote their own accounts of what it would have been like to be a child when those early communities were flourishing. They also gained confidence as they talked about their photographs and explained to their groups why they had chosen their various pictures. Considerable insight was shown as they offered constructive criticism to each other. Each school approached the project

Children at the Eastgate Centre. (© Bob Fisher)

in its own individual way, but soon displays of work were proudly exhibited on the walls of corridors. This increased the interest of pupils in other years. The project was under way.

The next stage of the work was to take the children out to walk various sections of the proposed Heritage Trail. Plans were made and minibuses booked. The best time to make these visits was thought to be the summer term. They had to be fitted in around all the many other activities that take place in schools at this time of year. Of course no one had any idea just how cold and wet the early summer of 2007 was to be! Fortunately, most of the days selected were reasonably rain-free as the excited groups set out, complete with cameras and note books.

Prize winners from all the schools with Hans Wusterfeld at the Eastgate Centre. (© Bob Fisher)

Cleaning the animal frieze. (© Bob Fisher)

There were walks through Gloucester Park, strolls through the market and exploration of the many interesting features scattered around the town centre and beyond. Cameras flashed as the children squatted down or stood on tiptoe to get the best possible shots. Bob Fisher and Vin Harrop were always on hand to give advice where necessary.

Each school walked their pre-selected section of the trail twice. The first time was a trial run to find the best shots and angles. On their return the children aimed to improve their original shots. The two visits gave each school the chance to have at least one visit in good weather.

The Eastgate Centre

The individual points of interest explored on the Heritage Trail will be mentioned in Chapters 3 and 4. However, the welcome given to the children at the Eastgate Centre must be included here. The manager, Hans Wusterfeld, arranged for each group visiting the town centre to pause by the moving Owl and the Pussiecat sculpture and receive soft drinks and crisps. Needless to say the refreshments were quickly disposed of by the young photographers!

Exhibitions and Awards

Early on in the planning stage of The Heritage Project it had been decided to run a competition to find the best photographs and pieces of writing from each school. In July 2007 the schools mounted their final exhibitions. The children made their own selection of the photographs and writing to be displayed. Then, two members of the team set out to judge the photographs while another pair judged the writing. This was far from easy. All the children had worked extremely hard, but finally the choices were made.

Once again Hans Wusterfeld allowed the Eastgate Centre to be used for an exhibition of the winners' work and on that occasion prizes were given. The first photographic prize winner in each school won a digital camera with the winning writer receiving a digital recorder. This could be used for interviews to help with future writing. From all the winners one overall champion in each discipline was also chosen. There was a more sophisticated camera for photography, awarded to Callum Smith of Bardfield Primary School, and a more advanced recorder for writing presented to Michael Pacey of Laindon Park Primary School.

Everyone agrees that the project so far has been a great success. The children have learnt new skills and we can only hope their interest in both photography and writing will continue into the future.

The project has also guided the children towards learning more about the past, present and future of Basildon and to become more aware of their own environment. Their help in creating a new Heritage Trail has been invaluable. As they looked for the best shots it was interesting to hear how often they complained about graffiti and litter spoiling the view. An awareness of such eyesores may well stay with these youngsters into adulthood and we can only hope that their pride in Basildon will continue and be passed on to future generations.

3

The Heritage Trail

Let's Set Out

The Lottery-sponsored Basildon Heritage Trail has been carefully designed to help those who follow it to learn more about the past, present and future of the town. It is a journey that can begin anywhere along the route, but for convenience in this book we will start at Gloucester Park. Certainly there is no need to attempt the whole trail on one occasion. Better to travel slowly, keeping eyes open and perhaps seeing the town in a new and very different way.

Gloucester Park

The park lies to the south of Cranes Farm Road and there is a large car park where the walk begins. The New Town planners realised the need for open spaces and the park was incorporated into their early designs. It is unusual to have such a large green space so close to the centre of the town, yet it is easy to forget that you are near to the bustle of shops and industry once you start walking under the many superb trees and along paths that lead to a tranquil lake. The Duke and Duchess of Gloucester officially opened the park in 1957 – hence the name. Since that time it has become a centre for sport and relaxation with its manmade hills adding extra interest.

The Murrayfield Pavilion

Turn west after the car park and go first towards the Murrayfield Pavilion. This was erected in 1967. At that time there were changing facilities, refreshments available and a scoreboard suitable for county-class cricket matches. Sadly the days when it was used for such events have long gone. The pavilion has fallen into disrepair. This has led to vandalism and the building is, at the time of writing, liberally decorated with graffiti.

Before moving on it is worth pausing to look towards the town centre. Once church spires and towers dominated the landscape in the British Isles, but here Brooke House can be seen rising above the trees, although it is also possible to catch a glimpse of the Bell Tower in St Martin's Square.

The sadly neglected Murrayfield Pavilion. (© Bob Fisher)

St Nicholas Church

To reach St Nicholas Church it is necessary to cross Upper Mayne using the underpass. Follow the road north, passing IFDS House until reaching Basildon Road on the left. Follow this road until arriving at Laindon Park Primary School. Church Hill goes past the school and soon you will see the church of St Nicholas on your right. This Grade I listed building is not always open, but it is well worth going up the steps and into the churchyard. From here there are amazing views southwards towards the New Town and to the north as far as the A127 and beyond.

As you stand at the bottom of the steps you can see the old wooden schoolhouse. This was supported by John Puckle, a local farmer, who bequeathed money to pay for a schoolmaster in the seventeenth century. The building may well have been used before this as a priest's house.

Inside the church there is the sense of peace that comes to a building that has been used as a place of worship and prayer for many centuries. The first recorded rector, Richard de List, was serving the church in 1254 and it is believed that the nave was already standing at that time. The wooden beams and fine organ are well worth seeing.

Leaving the church, St Nicholas Lane may be reached either by following a grass track through the trees, known as Hilly Road, or by continuing down Church Hill. At the bottom turn left and return to Gloucester Park. Once back in the park follow signs to the boating lake and the swimming pool.

Inside St Nicholas Church, Laindon, looking towards the altar. (© Bob Fisher)

The Lake

Turn south until you reach the lake. On the way, as you follow the path, it is quite a shock to realise how close you are to Upper Mayne. Standing by the lake and watching the many birds that nest in and around the quiet water it is easy to imagine that you are in the middle of the country. Canada Geese have taken up residence on the grass around the lake and frequently move onto the water, joining the many other wild fowl. The pupils of Laindon Park School found plenty of opportunities here to take interesting photographs from many different angles.

The Gloucester Park Swimming Pool

The covered and heated swimming pool was built in 1967 in the southern part of the park to a design by Kenneth Cotton. It is a championship-sized pool and there is also a teaching pool. The original plan was to build an Olympic-sized pool but it was soon realised that the construction costs would be prohibitive and admission charges would also be unreasonably high. The idea was therefore abandoned in favour of the less expensive pool. As greater headroom was needed over the diving platform and less at the shallow end of the pool a sloping roof was erected, with a flat one over the teaching area. A café and administrative offices were placed between the two pools, thus dividing the whole building into three linked elements. This is a fine example of a post-modernist building but its future is now in doubt as there are plans to create a new pool. (see Chapter 10)

Trees

100,000 trees were planted across Basildon by the Development Corporation, a far-sighted move that has helped to give something of a country feel to this densely populated town. Sadly around 6,000 elms were lost to Dutch Elm Disease in the early 1970s. Led by Henry Bradley the Corporation's landscape staff did everything they could to stem the spread of the disease, including the importation of tiny wasps said to be the deadly enemy of the Dutch Elm bugs. Unfortunately all efforts were in vain and by September 1973 local newspapers reported that the battle had been finally lost.

A Frieze of Animals

On leaving the park the trail continues by using the underpass beneath Broad Mayne. On either side of this tunnel there is a frieze of animals, designed by Wendy Taylor. Small children

The swimming pool beside a lake in Gloucester Park. (© Bob Fisher)

love to see how many they can identify and it certainly makes an interesting way to cross a very busy road. Next, turn sharp left and go up the steps leading towards St Martin's Square, the church and the free-standing bell tower. In 1996 there was a competition to find a suitable name for the square. This was won by a pupil from St Anne Line Roman Catholic Junior School.

St Martin of Tours Church

Consecrated in 1962 by the Bishop of Chelmsford, the church was designed by local architect Mrs Trena Cotton. (Her husband, Ken, was responsible for the swimming pool in Gloucester Park.) It is an impressive building, but with a tranquil beauty. The eye is immediately drawn to the plain east wall above the altar, dominated by a simple black cross.

Although a comparatively new church, St Martin's has links with the past. It was back in the thirteenth century that a Christian community was first established at the church of St Nicholas, Laindon, and it remained a place of worship through the following centuries. When the New Town came into being it was realised that another centre for Anglicanism was needed. Guided by the Laindon rector, the Reverend Bill Winfield, a new church was built in the town centre. The foundation stone was laid on 15 October 1960 by the then chairman of the Basildon Development Corporation, Sir Humfrey Gale.

The organ has an interesting history. Originally built in 1870 by William Hill it was placed in St Erkenwald's Church, Southend, in 1906 and was rebuilt and enlarged in 1959. When the church became redundant the Bishop of Chelmsford requested that the organ should be moved to St Martin of Tours Church. It arrived in 1980 and, with over 5,000 pipes and sixty-nine stops, it is regarded as one of the finest instruments of its type in the country.

The Stained Glass Windows
The magnificent stained-glass windows, on either side of the nave, were the work of Joseph Nuttgens and were installed in 1989 to celebrate the Silver Jubilee of the consecration of the church. Unlike those found in most traditional churches they reach up from floor level. Each bay cost £6,000 and the money was raised from Basildon District Council, local industry, Barclays Bank and the Ford Motor Company. In the Lady Chapel another Nuttgens window with the theme 'Queen of Heavens' shows symbols of the Virgin Mary in heaven. In the wall behind the altar a red light burns. There is a niche in the wall with a solitary red brick. Behind this is a small urn containing ashes from the crematoria at Auschwitz, a reminder of the need for understanding between people of different faiths and cultures. An Auschwitz Exhibition was held at the church in 1984 and the artist Jackie Hopwood used this as the inspiration for her Stations of the Cross displayed on the pillars of the church.

After the Second World War St Nicholas Church in Colchester was demolished but its sound lives on as its bells were donated to St Martin's Church.

Over the south porch, outside the church, is a representation of Christ. This unusual sculpture is of fibreglass. It was designed and constructed by T.B. Huxley-Jones. Sadly, within a few months of completion in 1968, the sculptor entered hospital with a heart condition. Just four days later he died, leaving this as his last piece of completed work.

One of the beautiful windows in St Martin of Tours Church. (© Bob Fisher, by kind permission of the vicar and PCC)

The fiberglass statue of Christ by T.B. Huxley-Jones. (© Bob Fisher)

The unique bell tower in St Martin's Square, the only one of its type in the world. (© Bob Fisher)

The Bell Tower

Built to mark the coming of the new millennium this unusual faceted glass-and-steel structure is a real addition to the town and reaches an impressive 85ft. It is a freestanding octagonal spire housing a peal of eight bells and includes over 300m of glass. The oldest, the tenor bell, was cast in 1441. This is unique, as it is the first bell in the world to be cast by a woman, namely Joanne (Joanna) Hille. Known as Basildon Bell Tower, it was designed by Douglas Galloway and the opening was a very auspicious occasion. It was on 12 March 1999 when Queen Elizabeth II arrived in Basildon for the opening ceremony.

St Martin's Garden

This beautiful garden is to be found on the south side of the church. It is an oasis of calm for those wishing to pause on a busy shopping day. Apparently it was originally planned as a scented garden, but climate change has meant that it is now more appropriate to have a dry garden.

The Basildon Centre, Towngate Theatre and Compass

After passing through the gardens, two large buildings can be seen to the north-west of the square. The Basildon Centre contains the town's administrative offices and the library. It was opened in November 1989. On the left is the very popular Towngate Theatre, which opened the previous year. This has bar areas and plenty of space for meetings and displays. These two buildings now form an essential part of the town's amenities.

It is worth stopping to look at the giant compass set in the pavement outside the theatre – an interesting feature often overlooked. It is most unusual as a person has to stand on the correct month marked in the centre so that his or her shadow can point to the correct time.

The Woodman

Across the square stands The Woodman. This statue was carved from a 200-year-old oak taken from the Langdon Hills. It is the work of a local sculptor, Dave Chapple. The children who visited this part of the Heritage Trail were fascinated by the work. Endless photographs were taken as they tried to see how many different animals had been carved around the main figure.

The Armillary Sundial

After leaving The Woodman it is necessary to cross Westgate and then follow the footpath to the right. At the end of the railings go down a sloping path leading to the Southernhay underpass. This takes the walker into Roundacre where the Armillary Sundial is located.

Designed by Wendy Taylor it was built by C & E Engineering under the watchful eye of Tom Wright, the managing director. As the work grew in size many doubted that it would be possible to get the completed sculpture through the foundry door. However, Tom had made his calculations with great care and when it was ready a crane was used to turn it on its side. It then passed through the door with just centimetres to spare. Police escorted the lorry bearing the work to the Roundacre site, where it was carefully dropped into place by a giant crane.

To The Town Square

Leaving Roundacre, return through the underpass and take the steps on the right into Southernhay. Turn into Fodderwick by The Moon on the Square and re-enter St Martin's Square. Walk on into the town square.

There are a number of points of interest in the town square. This is at the very heart of Basildon. The shopping area was essential to the developing town and it was built roughly halfway between the old centres at Laindon and Pitsea.

Barstable Cottage

It is hard to imagine as you stand surrounded by shops that this was once a place of green fields and country cottages. Marks & Spencer was built in such an area. This is where Hot Water Lane was once to be found. It has long since disappeared. One of the houses that was demolished at the time of the new development was Barstable Cottage. This was also known as Hotwater Hall, taking its name from the lane. Apparently manor courts were once held there and those who appeared before the magistrates were said to be in 'hot water'.

Detail from The Woodman carving. (Photographer Harry Skingle, aged ten, Laindon Park School)

The Armillary Sundial in Roundacre. Although this appears to be a quiet area to sit the roundabout above is always busy. (© Bob Fisher)

Like many properties of the time the cottage was built entirely of wood, apart from its brick chimney. There was no sink in the house and water came from a natural stream and was pumped up by hand. Before the property was taken over by the Development Corporation it was occupied by Ann and Walter James. Mr James was a skilled craftsman and he made many improvements to his home. He also kept animals, including pigs, goats and chickens. Many vegetables were grown and also tobacco plants as Mr James liked to cure and press the leaves.

Although the building was old and primitive the family loved it and it was a sad day when they were paid just £150 for their home when it was compulsorily purchased. Although they transferred to an old people's bungalow in Whitmore Way they were unable to settle. Eventually they moved away.

There are many other stories told of people who resented the new developments that replaced their homes, but realised too late what was happening. By the time they fully appreciated what was going on the opportunity to protest had passed. For many who were proud to have owned their own homes the amounts paid in compensation were so small that they would only buy a few pieces of furniture for their new rented accommodation. Sadly this even resulted in some suicides.

A Hidden Mosaic

High up on the wall opposite Marks & Spencer is a large mosaic. This is unfortunately mainly obscured by a canopy, so it is impossible to see it in its entirety. It was created by the artist Geoffrey Clark.

The town square with the Mother and Child statue and pool. This is a popular place for shoppers to pause. (© Bob Fisher)

Two Free Standing Buildings

The town square started to take shape in 1958. It is large and without the two imposing glass buildings in the centre it might appear plain and stark, as the shops are built in the angular style favoured in the late 1950s and 1960s. The first of these buildings houses Toni & Guy, one of the well-known hairdressing salons. Further along the square stands Costa, the coffee shop. On the pavement outside tables give the surrounding area a continental feel.

At one time Keay House jutted out into the square, but the front has now been reduced in size. The building was named after Basildon Development Corporation's first chairman, Sir Lancelot Keay. The mosaic mural on the house was the work of Anthony Holloway, although it was without a title.

The Town Clock and the Mother and Child Statue

Many shoppers fail to look up and so miss seeing the town clock. This circular design is at the top of a slim post and was installed in 1965.

A long, narrow water feature known as the Fountain Pool has, at its far end, the iconic Mother and Child statue. This was cast in bronze by Maurice Lambert in 1961. It has become the symbol of the town, representing the growth of Basildon New Town. If you look at the town crest you will see that it forms the central part and it is also incorporated in the mayor's chain of office.

Coins are often tossed into the water and, unfortunately, there is usually a collection of rubbish. Let us hope that a new sense of pride soon makes this a thing of the past.

Brooke House

No one visiting Basildon town centre can miss the mighty tower known as Brooke House. With fourteen storeys it dominates the skyline of the town square. Designed by Sir Basil Spence, noted for the twentieth-century addition to the war-damaged Coventry Cathedral, it is named after the former Housing Minister, Sir Henry Brooke. It is a Grade II listed building and is uniquely raised 8ft above the ground on eight 'V'-shaped reinforced concrete stanchions. This is currently the only housing unit in the town centre and it contains eighty-four flats. Like most tall buildings Brooke House moves slightly in high winds, but rather than being a defect this ensures that the building remains safe.

The unusual town clock. (© Bob Fisher)

Brooke House dominating the town square.
(© Bob Fisher)

Freedom House

Next to Booke House is the sunken square where the Post Office is to be found. On the corner of this square is Freedom House, with more shops protected by an overhang. On the south side of the building is an untitled tenor clef sculpture made in aluminium. This was the work of A.J. Poole and was erected in 1960.

Eastgate

The Eastgate Centre is well worth a visit by anyone coming to Basildon on a shopping expedition. Although the mall was built in 1985 the foyer, with its shops, escalators and mirror-like stainless steel, puts the complex very firmly in the twenty-first century.

A ride up the escalator brings you to Pussiewillow III, sometimes referred to as Pussywillow III, Pussiwillow III or Cat's Cradle. This amazing clock is the work of Rowland Emett, who was also responsible for the famous car in *Chitty Chitty Bang Bang*. It is a delight for children and adults alike as the various characters from *The Owl and the Pussy Cat* poem twist and turn as the clock chimes the hour, half and quarter hours. The work is 6m high and 5½m in diameter. Most of the construction is of small diameter steel or brass rods, steel wire and coloured sheet

The Eastgate Centre showing the impressive domed roof. (© Bob Fisher)

The Compass Bowl underpass. (© Bob Fisher)

steel. The whole feature stands on a podium, raising it above the floor so that it may be easily seen from a distance.

For two years Dennis Rookard worked in the Eastgate Centre as Father Christmas. The first year was at Sava Centre when he sat in a little grotto giving out presents to the children. The following year he was in the mall itself. This was a job Dennis really enjoyed. It involved six weeks' work from 10 a.m. to 5 p.m. The first day at the Eastgate Centre he arrived with a real, very friendly, reindeer brought down from Scotland.

The Compass Bowl

Designed by Wendy Taylor this interesting feature is, at the time of writing, sadly neglected. Built as a giant compass with the points marked on the ground and also on the walls, vegetation has flourished in this sunken garden. Creepers have grown to such an extent that some of the compass points are completely covered and stones on the ground are broken and need renewing.

4

The Heritage Trail Continued

Kingswood

Leaving the Compass Bowl it is now necessary to walk through the underpass before turning right into Nether Priors and then on into Kingswood. This is the part of the Heritage Trail that was first walked by the children from Pitsea Junior School.

Here you will see some typical 1960s houses. This must have been a fascinating project for the architects as they tried to make each house as individual as possible. Some of the trees have been pollarded, an unusual sight so close to a shopping centre. Looking back towards the town centre it is possible to see the blue-topped telephone exchange rising above the nearby properties.

Basildon (Barstable) Hall

By following Nether Priors, Clickett Hill will be reached. At the top of this hill a footpath on the right leads to houses facing an open space bordered on the far side by trees and bushes. This is where Basildon Hall stood until it was demolished during the development of the area in 1961.

The original hall was built prior to the compilation of the Domesday Book and it was mentioned in the records. At that time it was in the possession of Odo, Bishop of Bayeux. Later it was held by a son of Edward I, Edmund of Woodstock, Earl of Kent, so the manor had royal connections. A moat surrounded the hall and this remained until the new housing estate was well established.

Fire!

The house demolished in the early 1960s was not the original building on the site. By the 1830s the hall had become an inn. Apparently one day a lady arrived wearing a red cloak. She decided to spend the night at the inn. Another traveller placed a lighted candle in the top of a bottle that still contained some whisky. Time passed and the traveller fell asleep, forgetting about the candle. As it burnt down it fell into the bottle, which then exploded. The house was destroyed in the raging inferno that followed with both the lady and the careless traveller losing their lives. In time the house was rebuilt but it is said that the red-cloaked lady haunted the new building and

A class group from Pitsea School with Daphne Andrews. Mrs Andrews spent her childhood at Basildon Hall. A building had existed on the site since before the compilation of the Domesday Book. (© Vin Harrop)

she was seen on more than one occasion. There are also stories that the lady was seen at Holy Cross Church and dogs disliked passing the building. What connection, if any, she had with the church is unknown. However, some accounts tell of a ghostly monk.

Herman Gliessner

In the 1930s the rebuilt house was owned by a German, Herman Alwin Gliessner. He had lived in Basildon since before the First World War and farmed the land around the hall. It was by accident that he stayed in England at all. This was because he missed the ship on which he was serving when it sailed from London Docks.

At one point Mr Gliessner was interned in Frimly Internment Camp. It was during this time that locals ransacked the house, destroyed much of the building and set fire to what was left. Sadly vandals were around long before the twenty-first century. Eventually Herman Gliessner returned and rebuilt the house himself, before he moved away to Hill Road. He was an active member of the Basildon branch of the Residents Protection Association and later became its president. He died at the age of seventy-eight.

The filled-in moat that, for centuries, surrounded Basildon Hall. (© Bob Fisher)

New Tenants

Basildon Hall was let in 1942 to the Haywood family of Romford and the family stayed there until 1956. Fred Haywood had always wanted to own a smallholding. When he saw that Basildon Hall was available to rent he and his wife Mary decided that this would be the ideal place for them. They moved in with their children. In those days it was described as a lonely place standing in open fields. When their daughter, Dorothy, married, she and her husband also lived in the house and their first child was born there.

The hall must have been an idyllic place for growing children with its orchard, animals and moat for boating. In winter the moat was liable to freeze and if the ice became hard enough then skating was possible.

Of course there was also a downside – there was no electricity or gas in those days and water was drawn from a well, one of five on the site. Only two of them were considered fit for human drinking water, the others being used for the animals. There was also a standpipe at the bottom of the road, but this was only used on very rare occasions. A brick-built structure protected the pipe and only a few people had the key. Once buckets had been filled with water they had to be carried back up the hill.

Puck Lane showing 1960s housing and the wood. (© Bob Fisher)

A Disappearing Moat

In July 1952 an article in the *Southend Standard* was headed by a photograph of the house and its picturesque moat with the heading, 'This Scene Won't Change'. The moat was the subject of a Ministry of Works preservation order and was classified as an ancient monument. 'For this reason', the article stated, 'it is unlikely that the farmhouse will be pulled down'.

Just a few years later, in October 1961, another newspaper article showed the moat being drained. Apparently the new residents had complained about smells from the stagnant water, mosquitoes and mud-caked children. Previously roach, carp and sticklebacks had thrived in the moat. A corporation spokesman claimed that considerable amounts of rubbish had also been dumped in the water. It is certainly strange that, after hundreds of years, this previous beauty spot deteriorated so dramatically.

The moat was partly filled in and the banks landscaped, making an attractive open space. However, it remains an ancient monument. Today some of the trees, dating back to the time when this was farmland, still remain.

The Water Feature outside the Ford building. (© Bob Fisher)

Puck Wood

Leaving the remains of the moat behind, cross the bridge over the London to Southend railway line and continue into Puck Lane. This follows the line of a very old dirt track that would have been used by carts travelling beside Puck Wood on the right.

Cherry Tree School, formerly Swan Mead, is close to Puck Lane. This was the site of the discovery of a Bronze Age hoard, so the area must have been inhabited from very early times.

On one side of Puck Lane are houses and these overlook the ancient Puck Wood. The lane is often narrow and follows a winding route. In the wood wild flowers grow beneath the trees, giving a sense of peace. This is another welcome green lung that has been preserved since the building of the New Town.

Ford Connections

The lane finally reaches Clay Hill Road and the Heritage Trail continues, passing Kingswood Medical Centre and the Owl and the Pussycat. After the Kingswood Schools, Cherrydown East is entered where there used to be a Ford car showroom. This has now been replaced by a block of flats.

Basildon Railway Station, finally opened in 1974. (© Bob Fisher)

The Ford Motor Company. has played a significant part in the development of the New Town. From the early days of the new development the company decided that the town would be the ideal place to build their new tractor plant. This caused problems. The chosen site came in greenbelt land and the government had already decided that the plant should be situated in the north of the country.

Henry Ford disagreed. So determined was he to have the plant in the south that he flew over from the United States to put his case. A meeting was arranged between Mr Ford and a government minister. Following this meeting Basildon Corporation was ordered to agree to the development by the company.

As a result of these high-level negotiations the tractor plant was duly built in Cranes Farm Road and the opening took place in 1963. The cost at that time was £600,000. This was a very important decision for Basildon as the Ford Co. has had a considerable influence on the town.

At the end of Cherrydown East there is a sculpture known as the Water Feature. It is the work of William Mitchell. Following the Heritage Trail Trafford House is approached. Built in 1977 this building is another link with the Ford Co. Trafford Park in Manchester was where Henry Ford produced the very first Model T Ford car.

The Railway Station

The first railway line to come through the Basildon area had been built between 1851 and 1854. However, at that time the only stations were at Pitsea and Laindon. Trains passed between the two stations without pause, even when the New Town was increasing daily in size under ever-expanding development.

Delays!

A major campaign for a Basildon railway station dominated the 1960s. A suitable site was chosen, but progress was slow. This was in the days of the Beeching railway closures. Stations and lines were becoming redundant across the country. It was certainly not the time for the opening of new stations.

The Development Corporation backed the idea of a central station. This, they argued, was essential if the town was to continue to thrive. Commuters needed easy access to the railway and shop owners realised that a local station would bring more customers into the town. By June 1960 5,500 signatures had been collected by the Town Centre Shop Association on a petition asking for a station. This was sent to the Ministry of Transport. The petitioners may have been optimistic that their request would be granted. If so, their hopes were soon dashed. There was little response.

It was only after two years that the Council and the Corporation together sent a deputation to British Rail. They then discovered that they would only get their new station if the two authorities made a financial contribution towards the cost. They were also told that either Pitsea or Laindon Station would have to be closed. This solution was completely unacceptable so no further negotiations took place.

After several years the Development Corporation finally reached an agreement for a new station without cost to the ratepayers. A developer would be permitted to build a 271,000 sq. ft office block beside the railway. A deal was signed and work started on this construction in January 1973. Unfortunately it was still incomplete when the station was ready to open in November 1974.

The structure remained empty for some time. Then, in July 1977, the Ford Motor Company decided to take over the entire building. This was to be used as the headquarters of the firm's European truck operations and jobs would be created for 2,000 people. There was a snag. The company wanted car-parking facilities for employees during the week. This meant the loss of a large public car park to the south of the railway line, an agreement that later caused parking problems for those using the town centre. Nevertheless, the town now had its station and it is one that has been very well used in the years since its opening.

The Bus Station

The Trail now comes close to the bus station, opposite Market Pavement. This is dominated by a huge mosaic of the history of Basildon across the façade of Blenheim House. This eye-catching mosaic with its 16,000 hand-painted tiles is the work of John Gordon. From this point the glass Norwich Union building may be seen.

Basildon Market. (© Bob Fisher)

Pupils from Bardfield School visiting the market. (© Bob Fisher)

The Market

Markets have been an important part of social and economic communities throughout the centuries. In ancient Rome the citizens met to trade and gossip. Later, in the Middle Ages, the market played an essential part in the life of towns and cities across Britain. In more recent times many of the old traditional markets have disappeared, being replaced by supermarkets and cut-price stores. However, Basildon is lucky enough still to have a thriving market close to the town centre. Stalls first came into the area in the autumn of 1958 and they were welcomed by the newcomers who were delighted by the cheap prices.

Ten years ago Paul Dawson was appointed as the manager of the market. He has many years of experience, having started learning his trade as a twelve-year-old and that experience shows in this well-run trading centre. He recalls that many of the original traders used caravans for the purpose of selling their goods. Now most have more permanent stalls. In recent times green and white awnings have been added to many of them, giving a traditional feel to the complex.

A Visit to the Market
Pupils from Bardfield Primary School, as part of their pioneering work on the Basildon Heritage Trail, visited the market on a fine June day. The traders could not have been more helpful and welcoming. Rob Davis and Alexander Smith patiently answered questions about their colourful and well-stocked fruit and vegetable stall. The enticing smells alone must help to sell the produce.

They explained how they put out their wares between 5 and 7 a.m. and before that everything must be brought in from London.

Another greengrocer who welcomed the children was Jane Nowers. Her husband, Stephen, sets his alarm for 2.30 a.m. on market days in time to set off for London to buy produce. A visit to Steven Page's well-stocked fishmongers stall also proved popular with the children. The boys especially enjoyed examining the various types of fish being offered for sale.

For the girls Catherine Day's haberdashery stall was of special interest. Catherine has worked in the market for twenty years. Her goods are bought in Brick Lane in London. She explained how it takes four hours to set up the stall, although she does have two boys to help with this work.

Much to the delight of the children Paul Dawson presented them with certificates at the end of their visit to commemorate this very special day.

Linking the Present and the Past

After the market it is necessary to pass once more through the town square, East Square and East Walk, turning left to walk by Toys R Us and crossing Great Oaks at the pedestrian crossing by Staples, the office suppliers. Broadmayne, too, must be carefully negotiated before turning into Ghyllgrove. The name Audley Way on the left recalls the acquisition of the lands of the

Taken from the top of Brooke House, this photograph shows the fire station tower and the convex terrace. (© Bob Fisher)

The mural at the bus station shows the history of Basildon in pictorial form. Here we see the section for 1914. (© Bob Fisher)

Abbey of Walden by Sir Thomas Audley in 1538. This was in the time of Henry VIII, following the Dissolution of the Monasteries. Braybrooke, which is off Audley Way, is named after the first Lord Braybrooke who took over the beautiful Essex mansion, Audley End, in the late eighteenth century. He spent £100,000 on restorations to the house.

On the right is an interesting and unusual convex terrace of houses. We are more used to seeing the gracious inward curving Georgian crescents but this terrace dates from the early 1960s.

To the east of Ghyllgrove is Honeypot Lane, apparently taking its name from the thick, sticky London clay to be found there. Certainly there are reports that the road flooded regularly whenever it rained and in winter it was almost impassable. One winter, boats were said to have taken part in races there and cows were fed and milked in the fields rather than taking the risk of them becoming stuck in the thick mud as they moved to milking sheds. However, at least one source says that Beehive Lane, in the same area, once had hives there, so perhaps there is a more romantic reason for the naming of Honeypot Lane. It was in this area that the famous 1906 Basildon murder took place, mentioned in Chapter 2. Further north along Ghyllgrove, The Gore is passed. This name also has links to Essex history. The Gore was a farm in the Rochford Hundred. It was mentioned in the Court Rolls of 1374.

Next we come to Butneys on the left. From here there is a kissing gate leading into Gloucester Park.

Our journey following the Heritage Trail is now almost complete. As you pass along the winding path towards the car park pause to note the many superb trees and the manmade hills that add interest to what would otherwise be a very flat landscape. Park Meadow on the right is now a haven for wildflowers and insects. It is amazing to think how close this beautiful green space is to the hubbub of the thriving town.

Turn left after the footbridge and follow the signpost to the Athletics Stadium/Pavillion. There is then a short walk to return to the car park where the trail began.

Whether you follow the Heritage Trail in small bites or all in one go it is hoped it will help you to learn more about our fascinating, but often misunderstood, town of Basildon.

5

Cherry Tree Primary School

Five Very Special Schools

In the following chapters we will look at the five schools that took part in the establishment of the Basildon Heritage Trail. Each one makes its own very individual contribution to the life of the town. Here our future citizens are being encouraged to learn and develop by dedicated teachers.

A School Built on History

When workmen started digging the foundations for the first school to be built after the creation of Basildon New Town they were in for a surprise. They were employed on a site at the corner of Bull Road and Church Road. As a drainage trench was dug, some unusual objects appeared. The finds included a large collection of metalwork and fragments of ancient weapons dating from 800 to 700 BC – the Late Bronze Age. The finds were removed to safety and became known as the Vange Hoard. They are now to be found at the Southend-on-Sea Museum in Victoria Avenue.

The builders continued with their work until Swan Mead School (later known as Cherry Tree Primary School) was completed. It finally opened in April 1954. At the time of writing there are 322 children on the roll in thirteen classes with a fairly even balance between boys and girls. The number of children who have English as a second language is steadily increasing, adding further enrichment to the community. These children are quickly assimilated into their class groups. It is often easier for children to pick up a new language than it is for adults and this is the case at Cherry Tree School. The younger the child is on joining the school the more quickly he or she adapts to using two languages in their daily life.

Learning to Learn

Learning to learn is the school ethos. In the school prospectus six aims are listed:

- To set and realize the highest standards of teaching, learning, achievement and behaviour.
- To foster a love of learning, supporting and celebrating achievements.

Children from Cherry Tree School with their teachers. (© Bob Fisher)

A dedicated school governor, Richard Perry, helping with reading. (© Bob Fisher)

Tiles made in a workshop lesson by the pupils. (© Bob Fisher)

- To develop positive links with the local community.
- To value equally all cultures, faiths, languages and experiences.
- To ensure that all members of the school community contribute to the development of the school.
- To reflect these aims in day to day practice.

The school aims to exceed expectations.

A Changing School

It was in 2000-2001 that the school ceased to have separate infant and junior sections and the two parts were united. At the same time the name was changed from Swan Mead to Cherry Tree and a cherry tree was adopted as the new school badge.

Mrs Eileen Lynch, the headteacher, is very proud of both the children and adults who work in the school. It is four years since she first took up her appointment and in that time she has seen the children and staff working together as a team. There is now an increased sense of being a part of the community. Although this was once a failing school Cherry Tree is facing a bright future as it goes from strength to strength. This is a busy community, but there is a very friendly atmosphere.

A class group, *c.* 1960. (Cherry Tree School archives)

Trouble with Dogs

Children are always attracted to animals and when one wanders into a school playground there are bound to be problems. This happened in February 1969 when two dogs entered the school premises during the lunch hour. Whether they were teased or frightened is not recorded but apparently ten children were bitten, eight only slightly but two were sent home with recommendations that they should be seen by a doctor. It was noted at the time that the trouble was mainly the fault of the children themselves but a report was made by telephone to the police.

Problems!

An event still remembered in the history of the school occurred on the night of 1 November 1969. Somehow vandals managed to enter the building. The headteacher's office was ransacked and furniture was taken from the staff room to the hall. There it was burnt. The fire raged and part of the school was destroyed. As a result of this the whole building had to be closed. Staff went in to salvage what equipment they could and the children were moved to Northlands County Primary School. This must have reminded many of the war years when schools were forced to make space for evacuees and those who had been bombed out. It would have been a very sad time for all the children and staff involved. The school finally reopened in January 1970.

Arsonists hit again in January 1979. This happened in the school grounds late in the evening. Vandals set light to the Wendy House. Although the fire brigade arrived they were too late to save the structure, which must have been a great disappointment for the younger children.

Ofsted

The Ofsted inspection team visited the school in January 2005. After a number of problems in the past it was felt that real progress was being made. Overall everything was satisfactory and some areas were described as good with SATS results improving steadily.

To celebrate this encouraging news it was decided to plant a cherry tree in the school grounds. Also a circle of logs was arranged to encourage insects and small creatures – an excellent way to study nature.

Hungry Thieves

A spate of thefts over the years involved the removal of food. Just before Christmas in 1979 thieves broke in and took a number of items belonging to the staff. Later the cook discovered

Celebration plates made after the successful Ofsted inspection in 2005. (© Bob Fisher)

that the kitchen had also been entered and a large quantity of food had been removed from the fridge and freezer.

In April of the same year thieves returned and once again visited the kitchen. A quantity of frozen food was taken on that occasion.

At the end of the year the kitchen was yet again the focus of attention for thieves. This time the freezer was broken open, sausages were taken and then cooked, presumably without defrosting them first! Sadly the criminals also found a fire extinguisher and sprayed the contents over the floor and walls. They also left the freezer door open, thus making sure that the rest of the food had to be condemned. Twice in February of that year the kitchen was yet again targeted and a considerable amount of food was stolen. A jar of coffee was also taken from the staff room. Fortunately security is now very tight and is regularly reviewed. There is a coded security entrance to the school and the entire building is carefully monitored at all times.

The School Council

Cherry Tree has a flourishing School Council. From Year 3 up one child is elected as a representative from each class, so there are usually between ten and twelve members. When they meet they are given subjects to think about and they make decisions about what they would like to discuss.

Many useful ideas come from these meetings. Recently it was suggested that the school should start a recycling scheme. There had been workshops in school considering the importance of recycling and the children felt that they would like to make their own contribution. It was decided to collect clothes and shoes. Those involved had a lot of fun sorting through the clothes and putting them into bags. It was then arranged that a company would come to take away the goods and payment would be made.

£55 was raised and the Council members then had to decide how the money should be spent. After some discussion it was agreed that a bin should be bought for each classroom. Waste paper could then be collected ready for recycling. Although no money will be made from this project the children realise how important it is to avoid waste. Most children today know a great deal about global warming and the need to save the planet, but in this project they have a chance to make their very own practical contribution.

The Heritage Project

Mrs Lynch was most enthusiastic about the Heritage Project. She said that the children really enjoyed taking part. An exhibition of the work produced was set up in the entrance lobby and visitors to the school were most impressed by the standard of the work, especially remarking on the quality of the photographs and the very positive images recorded. The children enjoyed learning the new technical language involved as they discovered more about the use of the digital cameras. Once they had finished their work they managed to give constructive criticism to each other in a way that many adults find difficult. It was felt that this was a really worthwhile project.

An exhibition of photographs and writing showing work connected with the Heritage Project. (© Bob Fisher)

Music and Drama

The school has always been involved in music and drama events. The records show that in 1975 the top infant classes visited The Arts Centre Theatre in Basildon to see a performance given by The Children's Theatre Group. The following year the choir took part in the music festival at Brooklands School. Their individual item was a musical play, *Pussy Cat, Pussy Cat, Where Have You Been?* Other music and drama festivals have also been enjoyed over the years, including the Basildon Music Festival, and various groups have visited the school to entertain. When *The Wizard of Oz* was put on at the Towngate Theatre a group of Cherry Tree children had real stage experience as they were chosen to be munchkins.

Recently Cherry Tree has been part of a project to bring enough brass instruments into the school for one class to be taught at a time. Music is taught in lessons where the children have a chance to improve their knowledge in a number of ways. Percussion instruments are popular and the choir performs both in school and at outside concerts. Drama is enjoyed through clubs.

Children at work, c. 1960. (Cherry Tree School archives)

There is always a special concert at Christmas and one of the highlights of the year is the phenomenal summer concert. As many children as possible take part. Those who prefer not to appear on stage help with music, lighting, scenery and props. Parents come to watch and this really is an event to be enjoyed by the whole school.

Celebrations

Schools love to have a reason for a celebration. Harvest Festival, Christmas and Easter appear regularly in the record books, showing how often the school has used these events to raise money for charity. Money has been raised at a Harvest Festival for the Ghyllgrove partial hearing unit and many other good causes have benefited from the generosity of the Cherry Tree children and their families. At Christmas time there are concerts, carol singing and all the usual excitement as the holidays approach. There are also memories of Easter Parades, with hats made by the parents and children and of an Easter egg being given to each child.

In June 1977 it was time to celebrate the fact that the Queen had been on the throne for twenty-five years. What better reason could be needed to hold a party? Plans were made for the Silver Jubilee celebrations. Cakes were provided by the parents and School Fund money was used to purchase orange squash and ice cream. The same source was also used so that each child could be given a Jubilee Crown, a permanent reminder of a very special day. Luckily the weather

A view across the school playing fields. (© Bob Fisher)

was kind so the children played games on the grass and later there was a puppet show put on by one of the pupils and her older brother. In fact so many cakes had been provided that there were enough for the children to continue their celebrations over the next two days! There was also a special Jubilee assembly, conducted by the children.

Another Silver Anniversary

The school celebrated its own twenty-fifth anniversary on 9 May 1979. Although the original opening day had been 28 April 1954, this was the most convenient date to remember the momentous event.

The Palace Theatre Travelling Players arrived to entertain the children with a special play, *The Mysterious Dr Moffett*. Afterwards everyone enjoyed games on the school field before returning to classrooms for a party tea.

Fifty Golden Years

By 2003 fifty years had passed since the opening of the school. It was also the year when building work was completed joining the two existing buildings. The decision was taken to mark these two happenings with a week of special events starting on 22 September.

On Monday the author Antony Lishak visited the school. He gave the children tips on how to become an author and improve their writing techniques. After school he stayed behind to meet parents and sign copies of his books.

The following day was given over to a range of physical activities. Specialists arrived from Barstable and The Deans Schools to coach the children and encourage them to acquire new skills and improve those already learnt. By the end of the day there were very tired, but happy, pupils.

Wednesday was another exciting day with the focus on music. A drummer came to the school to work with the children. Then, at 2.30 p.m. there was a musical performance for the whole school in the entrance hall. Parents were invited to come along and enjoy the results of the day's hard work.

On Thursday children from Reception to Year 6 worked together in 'family' groups on cross-curricular activities. This must have been a fascinating experiment and was obviously enjoyed by everyone.

The last day of the celebrations arrived. This started with a whole-school assembly when the work produced during the week was displayed and experiences were shared. Following this there was a balloon launch. The idea was to fill the sky with blue balloons. The children had been encouraged to sell balloons at £1 each and the family selling the most balloons received Argos tokens. An *Evening Echo* photographer arrived to make a permanent record of this spectacular event.

Explaining Heritage Project work to the class. (© Bob Fisher)

A class at work, *c.* 1960. (Cherry Tree School archives)

The oldest New Town school had celebrated its half century in style. There have been many changes over those years, but Cherry Tree Primary School is on course to get stronger and more successful as the years go by.

Towards the Future

Mrs Lynch has high hopes for the future of the school. Supported by her enthusiastic staff she expects to see standards continue to improve and to nurture the strong sense of community that is developing at Cherry Tree School.

6

Bardfield Primary School

A Caring Environment for Thinking and Learning

Bardfield School first opened its doors to pupils on 6 September 1966. At that time 112 children were admitted, twenty-six junior boys and thirty-eight junior girls. There were also twenty-eight infant boys and twenty girls. These numbers included eleven reception children. Since then the school has flourished and the numbers have grown, until reaching the present total of 277, including the nursery children. This number fluctuates during the year as pupils move away and new entrants arrive.

Over the years there have been many changes. 2002 saw the Infant and Junior Schools amalgamated to form Bardfield Primary School under the leadership of the present headmistress, Mrs Yvonne Burgess. Mrs Burgess first joined the Infant School in 1996, moving to the Juniors in 1999 as acting headteacher and then becoming headmistress when the two sections of the school united.

The school motto is 'A Caring Environment for Thinking and Learning'. There is also a special logo – a mouse holding a pen. This was designed before the amalgamation and when the children were asked if they would like a new badge they asked to keep the old one. This is unique to the school as the pen stands for The Bard and the mouse is a field mouse. The designer of the logo was a former pupil of the school in the 1980s and she was invited to the opening of the combined school.

A Dedicated Secretary

Mrs Michelle Page first joined the school as a Welfare Assistant in 1986. She has seen how much the office work has changed since then. When she first came any mother who volunteered could come into the office to answer the telephone, stick on a plaster for an injured child or type a letter. Now the job has become very professional and qualifications are needed to be able to work there.

In those early days the office staff had almost nothing to do with finance. Their main job was concerned with ordering supplies. Now they are expected to do everything from coping with salaries and paying bills to dealing with any member of the public who enters the school.

Physically there have been changes, too. In 1992 Bardfield became a locally managed school for finance under the direction of Essex County Council. Until that time there had been a wire

The school badge. (© Bob Fisher)

mesh fence around the premises. The new management insisted that a proper fence must be erected around the site at a cost of £22,000! This had to be paid for out of the school budget.

So why has Mrs Page stayed at the school for so long? She says it is because it has such a caring staff. Although people come and go, concern for others seems to be passed on. When she was off sick for some time the staff kept in touch, made visits and phone calls and made sure that she was still involved. The school motto is one that touches adults as well as children.

There is also the pleasure of seeing past pupils return, sometimes as parents, and also the satisfaction of watching newly qualified teachers gain confidence and promotion. In fact some have gone on to become headteachers themselves. Many of the staff who have left still keep in touch.

A Warm Welcome

The school log book contains some interesting information about the early days of Bardfield's existence. We often complain about problems with builders, but this is nothing new. Shortly after the opening of Bardfield School in 1966 there were a number of teething problems. Plumbers were summoned on 19 September to repair waste pipes in the girls' upstairs washbasins. These had fallen off during the weekend. A few days later the main electricity supply to the kitchen failed. Later it was discovered that this was due to a faulty fuse in a sealed unit. Fortunately repairs were effected and the service was resumed in a little over an hour.

Early in October Miss Whenn, the acting headmistress, was faced with a problem of a different nature. Just before 10 a.m. Mrs Moody, the cook, reported considerable overheating of the fish fryer.

Mrs Page in her office. (© Bob Fisher)

It wasn't the first time this piece of equipment had caused problems so a call was put through to the Education Office so that the suppliers could be informed and urgent repairs undertaken.

A few minutes later Mrs Moody returned to report that 4ft-high flames were rising from the fryer, which had now been turned off! Miss Whenn attempted to turn off the electricity supply, but she was unable to locate the switch. At that point she decided to drive to the caretaker's house to see if he could help, having first left instructions that the fire brigade should be called. On arriving at the caretaker's house the acting headmistress discovered that he was out, so she left a message with his wife before returning to the school.

Two fire appliances arrived and their crews soon dealt with the problem. There was apparently no likelihood of the whole school catching fire, but it was deemed wise to send all the children out to play as a precaution. Nobody was hurt and there was no major damage, except to the equipment concerned.

Water, Water Everywhere

Another building disaster occurred in 1990 when contractors arrived to work on the school roof. All went well until one very wet night. Rainwater burst through the ceiling of one upstairs classroom. It then seeped through into the room next door. The water poured through the floor and the ceiling of the classroom below. This room was awash and part of the ceiling collapsed onto maths equipment and the cloakroom area.

Other classrooms were also affected. Some ceiling tiles were lost and displays of work ruined. Problems were also discovered in the downstairs toilets where a fuse box filled with water. This

Bardfield School, outside the two-storey building. (© Bob Fisher)

resulted in the electricity being turned off. Dampness was also found in the gents' toilets and in the dining room. As the headteacher commented at the time, 'Having almost ninety children in the hall area is not ideal!'

Music and Drama and Art

There is a purpose-built Art Block, incorporating a superb Music and Drama studio. At first there were two school buildings divided by a car park, but now the Art Centre unites them.

The importance of seeing professional productions is fully appreciated. A visit to the pantomime in Southend was a great treat. In fact, for a number of children, it was their first ever visit to a theatre. There is also an annual Christmas production and the Infant School puts on its own plays. Recently *The Polar Express* was their choice. Parents eagerly came into the school to see the finished performances.

Music has always played an important part in school life. When a television programme suggested that schools could send in videos of their choirs performing a song from *Joseph and the Amazing Technicolor Dreamcoat*, Bardfield took part with enthusiasm. Although they were not the school finally chosen, taking part was a valuable experience. The children have also been involved in the Basildon Music Festival and in 1989 Emily Dowling was named as a winner in the Basildon Writer of the Year competition.

Children in Victorian dress as part of a project. (Bardfield School archives)

Children working on a craft project. (Bardfield School archives)

A Busy School

Many special events are celebrated during the school year. There is an Art Week, a Maths Week and a Science Week when parents are invited into the school to see the progress being made in each subject. Book Week is also an important date in the school year when children can dress up as characters from books. Every week notable achievements of the pupils are recorded.

The main religious festivals are celebrated in assembly. Harvest Festival is one of these times. Following the school's first Harvest Festival in October 1966, the produce was sold to start the School Fund. Just over £16 was raised. Later that year every child in the school took part in the nativity play to which school managers, parents and friends were invited. In more recent times tinned food, packed in boxes, has been sent to Romania or to help the homeless

History projects have recalled Victorian times with the children dressing up in appropriate costumes. There has been a hobbies day and visits to Wat Tyler Park.

After studying the Vikings a longboat was built. This was used in an assembly before being taken onto the field and burnt in the traditional way. There have been talent competitions and a Kingswood adventure weekend when, among other things, walls were scaled, aerial activities undertaken, and archery and fencing tried.

The summer fete has always been well supported. This is when the children and their visitors enjoy all the usual fun events, including a bouncy castle.

A Building for the Community

In the evenings the building is used for various classes and courses. Some of these are run by the local Adult Community College. The Art, Music and Drama Studios are used for evening activities and this has become a very popular venue.

Community Service has also worked in the school at weekends, helping with decorating, digging in the gardens and collecting litter. This has made a big difference to the school and both those who work and those who enjoy the results are justly pleased with the improvements made.

The Tale of a Fish Market

In classrooms, corridors and the hall of Bardfield School there are laminated cards with pictures of fish and short sentences. To understand why we must move to the USA.

In Seattle there was a failing fish market. It was very near to closure when a businessman decided to take it over. His aim was to make it a big success and a major tourist attraction – an apparently impossible task.

He told all his workers that they must work to four important rules:

- You must choose your attitude every day when you came to work.
- You must make someone's day.
- Whatever you do you must do it well. Be present.
- Have fun!

The system worked. There is now a highly successful, thriving market visited by thousands of tourists and the happy atmosphere leads to far more fish being sold.

The school has adopted this 'fish philosophy'. At the moment they are working with a company called Eddison who introduced the idea to the school. The children were asked to decide what they thought were the most important qualities for the school. They chose Respect, Responsibility and Courage. They were then asked to write what they thought each of these words meant and their ideas are now printed on the 'fish' motto sheets. These show Bardfield's Code of Conduct:

- We care for and look after each other and our environment.
- We show respect by listening to everyone and listen to what they say.
- We are positive when faced with challenges.
- We are kind, thoughtful and friendly to each other.

The pupils are awarded certificates when they show that they have put one of these ideas into practice.

A fish collage in the school hall. (© Bob Fisher)

A Time Capsule

In February 2006 work was about to be started on the Key Stage 2 playground. (Key Stage 2 is for children aged between eight and eleven). At that point it was decided to bury a time capsule that would then be covered by the intended work. The children discussed what should be included to give a snapshot of their lives on that date. In the end they chose to include various activity photographs, a staff list and a list of children on the roll, a school baseball cap, an *Evening Echo* article, the school newsletter for February 2006, coins of value from 1p-£2, pictures of favourite sweets and a tea towel. Also there was headed note paper, a cardigan with the school logo, a book bag, children's drawings, an internal plan of the school and lunch menus for 20 February 2006. Finally the official UK singles chart for that week was added!

Snow!

Global warming is now blamed for every anomaly in our weather. However, looking through the school records it is obvious that unusual conditions are nothing new.

On the night of 11 January 1987 heavy snow fell. By morning it was still falling and the decision was made to close the school. Essex Radio broadcast the news of the closure at 7.45 a.m and as many staff as possible were notified by phone. Mrs Sharp, the cleaner in charge, had managed to get in and she manned the office and informed any parents and children who arrived of what had happened.

Later some intrepid kitchen staff tried to enter the school, but the snow had reached a depth of 2ft so access was impossible. Most schools in South East Essex also closed and traffic on many roads was at a standstill. Parts of Southend and Billericay were completely cut off. The school finally reopened on 19 January, but only after the headteacher had organised a snow clearing party.

Wind!

Friday 16 October 1987 was another date when weather took over and the school was again forced to close. Hurricane winds had affected the south and south-east of the country overnight. Trees were down, roads blocked and many buildings badly damaged by the gales. At 7 a.m. the school keeper phoned the head teacher to report that the electricity had been cut off and there was no heating in the building. A large tree had also fallen blocking the children's entrance. Hasty telephone calls were made between the school keeper and the heads of the junior and infant schools and the decision was made to close both the schools.

New problems were faced. It was almost impossible to contact staff as phone lines were congested or out of order and it was too late for an announcement to go out on Essex Radio. However, national radio gave out frequent bulletins advising people to stay at home. Notices were posted outside the building advising anyone who did arrive of the closure. Happily there appears to have been no major structural damage to the school at that time.

Pausing by the Mother and Child Statue in the town square. (© Bob Fisher)

Food!

In 2007 the cost of a midday school meal reached £1.55 per day, although those with difficulties may apply for help. Packed lunches may be brought instead and these are transported in named boxes. It is also possible for the children to buy a biscuit or some fruit at morning break time and cartons of milk are also available. However, it is advised that only one item of tuck should be taken each day so that appetites are not affected at lunchtime. The Foundation Stage and Key Stage 1 children (those aged between four and seven years) are involved in the Government's Fruit and Vegetable scheme for Healthy Schools.

Looking Back

Reading through the school log books it is possible to see the way in which some things have changed over the years, but others have remained the same.

In March 1972 Mr Bungay, the Chief Education Officer, paid an informal visit to the school. He met the teaching staff, visited all the classrooms and stayed for lunch. Apparently he was highly satisfied with the tone of the school and complimented all the staff on the work being done. In the same month it was confirmed that approximately forty-five new houses were to be included in the school catchment area. These would all have three or four bedrooms, so there would be a considerable influx of new pupils to be accommodated in the summer term. By January 1976 the number on roll had increased to 205 boys and 166 girls.

The Heritage Project

It was a real pleasure to come into Bardfield School and to work with the staff and members of Year 5 on the Basildon Heritage Project. Their enthusiasm was obvious as they discovered how to use the digital cameras and to write about the images created. It was impressive to see how well they were prepared when they were taken to visit the market as part of their journey around the Heritage Trail. Their many questions were well thought out and their photographs caught the atmosphere of a busy market. Bardfield pupil Callum Smith was the overall winner of the photographic competition.

Ofsted

It is always a difficult time for teachers when it becomes known that an inspection is about to happen. Ofsted has now replaced the old inspections and Bardfield was one of the schools visited in 2007. The comments made were impressive and all those involved must have felt very pleased with the results. The school Prospectus includes some previous comments by Ofsted:

- 'The school has high expectations of the attitudes and behaviour of all its pupils.'
- 'Pupils' good attitudes and behaviour, supported by good relationships and personal development, significantly facilitate the school's calm and purposeful learning environment.'

Callum Smith's prize-winning photograph. (Photographer Callum Smith, aged ten)

- 'Pupils are prepared well for the next phase of education and to take their place in society as responsible citizens.'
- 'The school has clear aims and values that are reflected strongly in its work. There is a strong emphasis on developing a caring environment in which pupils feel secure and able to reach their full potential.'
- 'Staff treat their pupils with respect and give all pupils, regardless of their ability, gender or race, opportunities to be successful in their work.'

The Visitors' Book

Many people visiting the school leave comments in the Visitors' Book. Art Solutions spent four days working with the pupils in November 2006. At the end of their stay they said, 'What a fantastic school Bardfield Primary is. We have been so impressed with the behaviour we have seen during our four days working with you all. The children are delightful and so friendly and willing to help one another and ourselves. They show consideration for each other and for their school. They are a credit to Bardfield. It is obviously the result of all the hard work and dedication shown by all the adults in the school. We have really enjoyed our time with you. Thank you.'

Learning to use the cameras. (© Bob Fisher)

Another comment came from the Youth Sports Trust visitor Barry Howard. He said, 'I have been made very welcome at Bardfield by staff, pupils and in the staff room. The school's attitude towards outdoor education has been outstanding. An enjoyable five weeks for me and hopefully productive for Bardfield.'

There are a number of other encouraging comments and these show clearly that everyone in the school takes seriously the code of conduct on the motto sheets around the school.

Moving On

The majority of children from Bardfield School will move on to Barstable School for their secondary education. There are links with this and other feeder schools for children in their final primary year, with visits to and from the schools. This helps to ease the transition from one

Pupils using computers, *c.* 1990. (Bardfield School archives)

school to another. When the time comes to move on there will be some apprehension, but the children are well prepared for the future and should quickly fit into their new environment.

7

Laindon Park Primary School

The School Aims

We aim to provide a secure environment where children realise their full potential, develop responsibility and a long love of learning. The school encourages these values through an atmosphere of tolerance, equality, self worth and respect, offering a broad and balanced curriculum. The staff and governors of the school are committed to raising standards of achievement for all pupils in the school.

A School with a Past

Laindon Park Primary School has its roots in the past, but it is also very much a school of the twenty-first century. Built close to St Nicholas Church, at the top of Church Hill, the school first opened its doors to pupils in 1876 and is the oldest of the five schools taking part in the Basildon Heritage Project.

There was an earlier school close by, mentioned in Chapter 3. This was held in a small room measuring approximately 11 x 15ft at the back of St Nicholas Church. There may, at times, have been as many as fifty children being educated in this space. The building was possibly not originally built as a school. It was often referred to as 'The Priest's House' and may well have been where the curate lived. However, around 1617 a local farmer, John Puckle, endowed land to the church so that a schoolmaster could be employed to teach poor children from Basildon and Laindon.

Exactly when the extension that housed the school was built is open to debate but it has two floors above the former schoolroom, the first floor possibly being used by the children for recreation and the top for six Basildon (rather than Laindon) boarders. The reason for this distinction is unknown.

The last schoolmaster in the church school was James Hornsby who taught there for forty-eight years and retired as the nearby Laindon School was ready to open its doors as a Board School. He then moved to Church Road, but his working life was far from finished. He became a tax collector. James is buried in the churchyard with his three wives, one with him and the other two in the next grave. These graves are close to the old schoolhouse where he worked for so long. His name lives on at the nearby Hornsby Woods. The James Hornsby High School, which can be seen from the church, also recalls this early schoolmaster.

St Nicholas Church, Laindon, with the old wooden schoolhouse at the back. (© Bob Fisher)

The old building looks and feels like a village school. (© Bob Fisher)

A Village School in a Town

When the original Laindon Park School opened in 1876 on the present site it had just three classrooms leading onto an open corridor. This must have seemed real luxury after the conditions in the old schoolhouse. It is believed that this was the first purpose-built school in Basildon. At one time it was known as 'Donaldson's', taking its name from the headmistress at the time.

Although the school has grown since those early days, having had various extensions and alterations over the years, it still retains the feeling of a happy, welcoming village school. There is a small nursery class called Noah's Ark. Once they have passed their third birthday, children can join, if and when space permits. Here the young pupils start learning through play in a most attractive environment. Their room was once the school hall at a time when there were far fewer pupils than today. Many of the original features have been retained and the high ceiling and attractive windows help to make this a very welcoming centre for little learners. At the time of writing there are 107 children on the roll in the main school, plus a few in the nursery.

In recent years the school has grown and there are now five classes, excluding the nursery. Depending on numbers, class arrangement varies from one year to another. At the moment there is Reception/Year 1, Year 1/2, a separate Year 3, Year 4/5 and Year 6. Some families living in the catchment area tend to be mobile, although if it is possible many parents prefer to keep their children in the school, even if this means travelling. Although there are movements over the year generally the overall numbers remain fairly constant.

A Building that has Grown

Viewed from outside the building still retains its village-school appearance, but inside there have been many alterations. The open corridor was later enclosed and in the 1920s and 1930s a wooden extension was added, giving two more classrooms. The secretary's office was once in what is now the headteacher's office. Glass doors at the back of this room led into the headteacher's room and from this the schoolhouse could be reached through another door. This is where the headteacher would have lived, so the holder of that office was always on hand in case of emergency. The two-storey building now contains the staff room.

Building alterations are not just a thing of the past. For a number of years cracks appeared in the walls of the detached school hall. As long ago as 1989 these cracks were apparent, especially in the kitchen area. They were filled in and plastered but these were short-term remedies. There were plans at that time for the hall to be demolished and a new one built. This area also houses the kitchen and the main space is multi-purpose, being used for PE lessons, school meals, assemblies and many social functions. This is the last Horsa building in Essex, but it is finally to be demolished and a new hall is under construction and should open in 2008. The site of the old one will then become a much-needed playground. There is a playing field on the other side of Church Hill, but there is no room on the main site for further development.

Noah's Ark, the nursery held in the old school hall. (© Bob Fisher)

The original school door, still in use. (© Bob Fisher)

A Multicultural Mix

Some children arrive at the school without any knowledge of English. Recently there have been arrivals from Spain, Germany, Sudan, Ghana and Zimbabwe. However, it is found that the young children learn quickly from others who are only too keen to help. This is especially the case in The Ark. Here children love anyone who is different and will chatter happily to the newcomers, who quickly learn to respond. There are also books available written in the pupil's own language and these can be borrowed so parents are also able to encourage at home.

Special days from a variety of cultures are celebrated in assemblies, as well as the main Christian festivals. The school tries to run a multicultural and informative curriculum and children from different backgrounds are encouraged to share their knowledge with others.

Doors!

When visiting Laindon Park School it is interesting to pause for a few moments by the door that leads into the two-storey part of the building. This is original. One can only wonder how many hands have touched the aging wood over the years and what stories those red-painted planks could tell!

It is recorded that the summer of 1989 was very hot and that caused various problems to the school doors. The internal kitchen door became very difficult to unlock and the catch on the

Inside the Horsa hall. (© Bob Fisher)

boiler house would not work. Then, as the cleaners were leaving the building, they discovered that another external door could not be locked. When the headmistress arrived, she tied up the door with string! The police were notified, but it was the headteacher's husband who finally saved the day. He removed the brass plate from the door and that allowed the lock to function, although not very well. It was a few days before a blacksmith arrived to repair the damage but the building remained safe.

It was on 14 December 1989 that another problem lock was discovered. This was on the night of the school concert. The entertainment was a great success, but when the time came to close the back door into the hall it was found that the lock no longer worked. By that time a number of cracks had appeared in the walls of the building, so possibly movement had altered the door fitting.

The police were informed, but no action could be taken that night so the resourceful headteacher had PE equipment pushed against the door to form a very effective barricade. This was left in place over the entire weekend as no one was available to mend the lock until Monday. The headteacher returned on Sunday to check that all was well. How much easier it must have been to watch over the school in the days when the schoolhouse was still in use!

At the end of term the headteacher was leaving. However, she returned to the school on 27 December to clear out her remaining possessions, only to discover that the main door could not be locked. Calls to the Education Office were to no avail but help came on the following day. Fortunately modern security systems and locks mean that such problems are now well in the past.

An early photograph of a school group, *c.* 1900. (From Laindon Park archives)

The Tale of a Moth

In July 1990 an unusual problem arose. The end of term was approaching when the police called the headteacher to the school one evening. The security alarm had gone off, but the two attending police officers, after searching diligently, could find no sign of a break in. It was assumed that the alarm must be faulty. It was only the next morning that the cause of the problem was discovered. A moth had been trapped in the kitchen and had somehow managed to trigger the alarm system!

Charities

The children work enthusiastically for charity. One cause they supported recently was Barnardo's. As part of their fundraising they were asked to take part in a concert at the Royal Albert Hall. This was a great experience for all those involved. The final performance was open to the public and parents were able to see their children take part. There is not a separate school choir at the moment. This is such a small school that children volunteer to take part as the need arises. There is not a music specialist in the school at the time of writing, although a musician does visit the school to help with special musical activities.

Little Havens Children's Hospice has also been a charity supported by the school. For the past two years they have joined others to sing carols at the Eastgate Centre to raise money for the hospice. Following the Harvest Festival some gifts have been sold in support of Little Havens.

Sport

Because of the size of the school it is quite difficult to raise teams in any one age group. Children volunteer to take part in matches and those involved may be boys or girls and they range across the age groups. Obviously this puts them at a disadvantage when playing schools with first and second teams, but it is always emphasised that team spirit is far more important than winning. This attitude had certainly paid off because those who have taken part in rugby matches have often been complimented on their sportsmanship. Mrs Garland, the headteacher, has been in the school since 1998 and she feels that their small numbers are, in some ways, an advantage. If there are elite groups in a school then some keen children will never be picked. When you rely on volunteers everyone has an equal chance.

Nineteen Years of Service

Mrs Caroline Brand, a teaching assistant, has worked in the school for nineteen years. She has seen many changes in that time, but feels that it has grown ever more welcoming with the passing years. When she first arrived there was no nursery. Then, when it was first opened, it was to be found at the far end of the building, before moving to its present attractive location.

In those nineteen years Mrs Brand has seen the children develop far more self confidence and there is an increasingly open feel to the school. At one time parents felt that they must leave their children at the school gate and come no further. Although we now live in a time of ever-increasing security consciousness, nevertheless parents are welcomed into the school and there is a member of staff who has special responsibility for liaison with parents. In fact many come in regularly to help with reading, something that is much appreciated.

Memories from the 1980s and 1990s

Problems arise in all schools from time to time. In October 1989 the heating was turned on. Unfortunately it seems to have caused more problems than it solved. Some classrooms became much too hot, but others remained extremely cold.

At that time the harvest link was with Ramsdon Bell House Methodist Church. The minister arrived for the festival service with his guitar. He told the children a story and then sang to them to his own accompaniment. The food was displayed with the help of Year 3 and the next day it was collected by members of the WRVS for distribution to needy people in the district.

Volunteer groups of ladies also came into the school regularly to give help with sewing lessons.

Strong winds caused problems in January 1990. Overnight the weather changed and the next day it was too windy to allow the children outside at playtime. The following day the headteacher received a phone call at home at 7 a.m. saying that several areas of the school were without electricity, as a power line had been damaged during the bad weather of the previous evening. It was discovered that one fuse had blown, but there was still heating and light in the hall and kitchen so some work was able to continue that day.

Pupils using the cameras in Gloucester Park. (© Bob Fisher)

A Very Special Badge

The school badge shows two children and was actually designed by the pupils. At one point it was wondered if it should be altered, but the children wanted to keep it. It is certainly unique among school badges.

Ofsted

There was an Ofsted inspection early in 2007 and the results were most encouraging. The final report pointed out that the Victorian building is very well maintained and provides a bright, welcoming learning environment. In 2006 the SATS results showed improvement, with results in mathematics and science being above average.

There is very strong support in the school for children with special needs. Small classes and numbers on the roll mean that these children can receive concentrated help in areas where they have problems.

The Basildon Heritage Project

The children who took part in the Heritage Project approached their work with great enthusiasm. They obviously enjoyed their lessons with Bob Fisher, learning the secrets of digital cameras, and they used their new skills to take some very professional-looking photographs.

Mrs Garland felt that they had developed more of a sense of involvement with the town where they live as they viewed it through the camera. They became aware of graffiti and litter that spoil the environment and ruin a good photograph. Through this they realised that if you want to live somewhere nice then you have to look after that place. It also taught them that if you do not like something in your town then you can make a difference. It is no good waiting for someone else to effect changes.

Linking with their work on the project the children also made a study of the history of their school. All the children were involved in this work and they found out some very interesting facts as they delved into the past. The project continued over two terms and some of the photographs taken helped to enhance the finished results.

Laindon Park School badge designed by pupils. (© Bob Fisher)

The exhibition of work from the Heritage Project. (© Bob Fisher)

At the end of the summer term an exhibition was held in the school hall of all the photographs and written work that had been produced during the visits of the Heritage members to the school. They took real pride in this display and the overall winner for writing, Michael Pacey, came from Laindon Park Primary School.

Updating the Computer Stock

It was in March 1992 that the school received a telephone call from Mr Gerry Dunn, chairman of the London Taxi Drivers' Fund for underprivileged children. He offered £1,100 for the purpose of updating the school's computer stock. Needless to say this offer was gratefully received!

Later in the same year Class 3 took part in an Edwardian project. Someone came from the Essex Resources Centre to photograph the children at work. Edwardian costume was worn and a mock-up of a classroom from that time was made in the lower hall. Then some of the girls staged a protest concerning Women's Suffrage in the playground with banners and posters. This obviously made for an enjoyable and memorable day for all those involved and doubtless a great deal was learned about education in those faraway times.

Frances Clamp reading Michael Pacey's prize-winning story. Michael is fourth from the left. The photograph also includes John Jowers, Essex County Council cabinet member and Vin Harrop. (© Bob Fisher)

A School with a Future

Laindon Park is a school with an interesting past. There are problems to be faced in the twenty-first century with small numbers and a frequently shifting population. However, the hardworking and friendly staff create an atmosphere in which children are able to gain confidence and face the future with a positive attitude.

Small numbers mean that the children will not always win when they take part in competitive sports and music festivals, but instead they learn the importance of taking part and showing sportsmanship, qualities that will serve them well throughout their lives.

8

Pitsea Junior School

A Playground Senses Poem

I touch the red bricks,
The school's bare skin,
I hear the teachers murmuring,
Somewhere deep within,
I smell a faint smell,
Of pollution in the air,
I taste a bitter taste,
Spreading everywhere,
I see the teacher reaching,
The whistle to her lips,
While we go back to class
Occurs today's playtime eclipse

Joe Middleton, aged eleven

A School with a History

Pitsea School first opened its doors to pupils on 1 March 1909, having been built to serve the village community of Pitsea. Two full-time teachers were appointed to care for eighty-six students. A pupil teacher was also on the staff.

Much has changed over the years, in the town and in the school, as both have grown in ways that would have been unthinkable in those early days. There are, at the time of writing, 178 on the roll in the junior school with seven mixed-ability classes looked after by eight full time teachers, nine learning support assistants and also Mrs Alison Blant, the headteacher.

How different it must have been in those early days. The original plans show a two-storey building in the centre, with a ground-floor classroom on either side. Since then much building work has taken place. There is now an attractive red-brick building surrounded by extensive grounds. However, the early building remains, having been carefully incorporated into later plans.

Outside the original two-storey building. (© Bob Fisher)

Working Together to be Better

Although this is a busy, active school there is a feeling of calm when you enter the building. The children move around quietly, but with a sense of purpose. Mrs Blant believes that this is helped by the fact that, since the extensions, the school is built around two quadrangles. This means that classrooms are only on one side of the corridors, with large windows on the other side looking out onto tranquil gardens. This avoids the chaos that is often caused at the change of lessons when children come out of doors on both sides of a corridor.

Pitsea is also a school that was built before open-plan classrooms became popular, so no class is disturbed by another. This atmosphere is also nurtured by the headmistress and her staff who believe strongly in their motto, 'Working Together to be Better'. This motto was chosen by the children and teachers who tried to decide what the school was really about. They jointly came to the conclusion that they were aiming to be the best possible.

Weather Problems

In the days when the school first opened many of the old farms had been sold and the first wave of land agents had already started selling off small plots in the area. The majority of roads were unmade and those early settlers had none of the amenities we now take for granted. Water, gas, electricity and drainage were not available to most of the new shacks that were springing up. Although many only came at weekends, the new development must have affected the whole population.

In the first week only 87 per cent of the children on the roll attended. A severe snowstorm was blamed for the low numbers. In July of that year low attendance was also blamed on bad weather and the presence of the Fleet at Southend – an excuse that would not be acceptable today.

There were a number of reports of the weather affecting the attendance records. In January 1910 it was noted that severe flooding of the nearby roads made it impossible for children to reach the school on several occasions. A heavy snow fall was blamed for the bad attendance in April 1911. In September 1914 the woodwork teacher sent a telegram to the school saying that he was unable to attend due to inclement weather! One wonders how he managed to reach the post office to send his message.

A Busy School

Today there are interesting projects and activities that really encourage children to attend school, whatever the weather. Apart from the normal curriculum there are many clubs, both before and after school and also in the holidays. As the children join in with the different activities they gain new experiences and become better equipped to deal with life.

Each year the school takes part in a music festival and the children also participate in the District Sports. Year 6 pupils have the chance to go on a residential course in Wat Tyler Park. They do not have far to travel for this experience, meaning that the cost can be kept to a minimum so the maximum number of children can participate. Here they have the excitement of sleeping in dormitories and can even enjoy a midnight feast. They learn to work together in teams and are also able to enjoy barbecues, campfires, a witches walk and a haunted house. There may be little sleep during those few days but some very happy and contented children return at the end of the experience with memories that will last throughout their lives.

Special Days

Special days have always been celebrated in the school. Back in 1909 the school records show that Empire Day, 24 May, was a very important event. Special songs were sung in the morning and the Revd Hutton addressed the children. However, of even greater importance to the young pupils must have been the fact that the school closed at noon so that they could enjoy a half-day holiday. In July of the same year the school closed twice for what is recorded as 'Village Treats'. What form the treats took is not mentioned.

Today, special occasions are still celebrated, although in rather different ways. The school year starts with a friendship week. New children learn how to make friends and deal with the problems caused by old friends falling out. Two of the Year 6 pupils decided that they would also like to make a booklet to be given to those entering the school. This tells the new arrivals about their new school from the child's point of view. The young authors say it is a 'cool' place to be and one they obviously enjoy.

Mrs Blant in her office. (© Bob Fisher)

A Harvest Festival service is held in the autumn term at St Gabriel's Church and afterwards the produce is given to homeless people and also to elderly neighbours living close to the school. Christmas is celebrated with a concert on two evenings.

Easter sees a special assembly with seasonal hymns and there is also an Easter egg raffle.

Other Important Events

Each term a charity is chosen. This is often suggested by the children and they then raise money with enthusiasm. There are also special days and weeks. Science is a very important part of the curriculum and the school holds a Science Day when pupils join in a wide range of science experiments. There are also visits from teachers in the local secondary school who help the older children prepare for their move into senior education.

Writing Week is also an important event. This often corresponds with World Book Day. Children dress up as characters from their favourite books and published writers visit to encourage an interest in writing.

At the end of the school year there is a talent show, much enjoyed by everyone. The Leavers' Assembly is also a memorable and very positive event. One chapter in the life of the pupils is ending, but a new and equally exciting one is about to begin.

The netball team, *c.* 1960. (Pitsea School Archives)

Health

Health and Safety Week helps the children to learn more about personal hygiene and general safety issues. Road safety, awareness of stranger danger and many other important topics are covered. A nurse usually visits to talk about various health-related topics.

Most of the children walking around the school today look healthy and well fed. This was not always the case, as the school records show. Poor attendance was not simply caused by bad weather and road conditions. Illness also played a part, with childhood complaints passing rapidly through the school population.

A number of medical inspections were recorded over the years. In 1916 one child was found to have a squint and hearing problems, although it was thought she might not be able to hear at all. Another had broken his glasses and needed a new pair and many were found to have decayed teeth. During the same inspection one child had anaemia, another suffered from enlarged tonsils and adenoids and hospital treatment was recommended, and yet another needed an operation for a hernia. More squints were reported, head lice were found and there was some malnutrition.

Moving on to 8 November 1926, attendance was again low, this time due to inclement weather and some cases of mumps. A few days later, both mumps and chickenpox were reported

Pupils taking photographs. (© Bob Fisher)

as being on the increase and the facts were reported to the Ministry of Health. By the 25th of the month even more cases had been found and attendance had dropped to 63.5 per cent. By 6 December the epidemic had worsened even more with 50 per cent of the pupils being absent with mumps or chickenpox. Matters seem to have improved after Christmas when the school returned to normal.

By January 1944 attendance was badly affected by an outbreak of whooping cough and a mild attack of chickenpox. However, after the war there appear to have been fewer problems recorded than earlier in the century.

War

The outbreak of war in 1914 quickly affected the number of male members of staff available for teaching duties. Mr H. Okenden left on the morning of 18 September 1914 for military training, having enlisted in the Old Public Schools and Universities Men's Corps. In November of the same year woodwork classes were again cancelled, this time because Mr Baxter had been called up to serve in His Majesty's Forces. When war ended on 11 November 1914 the school closed for the afternoon in celebration.

Gathering clouds of war again affected the school in September 1939. It should have reopened on 4 September, but this finally happened on 23 October. At that time a shift system was introduced with children from Standard 2 upwards having classes from 8.45 until 11.30 a.m., with Standard 1 and the Infants attending from 12.40 until 2.45 p.m. On that first day only 50 per cent of the children attended. Staff numbers had also been reduced. Mr Bebington left because he had been called up for military service and Miss Hayward also ceased teaching because she had married during the vacation.

Outside the school building. (© Bob Fisher)

By November some problems had apparently been resolved and the school reopened to its full extent. The situation worsened in September 1940 when lessons were disrupted by incessant air-raid warnings and a great deal of time was spent in the shelters. Mr Stones left to report for military service.

Later in September the school was reported to be without gas. This meant that it was impossible to continue with dinners. It therefore became necessary to discharge the cooking staff until such time as gas once more became available. Apparently part of the school was also taken over to house a number of families who had been removed from their residencies owing to the proximity of unexploded time-bombs. In February 1944 the school hall was used as a centre for homeless people following a night of severe bombing.

Finally, in May 1945 the clouds of war lifted and the school closed for three days of celebrations for VE Day.

Music

Music has always played an important part in the life of Pitsea School. As long ago as 1923 the school was closed because the choir was competing in the Essex Schools' Music Festival. This was held in Romford. Whether or not those not actively involved attended is not recorded. However, we do know that the singers were awarded third prize in Class 2 of the Music Competition. In June 1939 thirty children attended the South East Essex Music Festival held at Leigh-on-Sea. The school does not appear to have closed on that occasion. In May 1983, twenty-eight children and two teachers went to Baddow Comprehensive School for a day called 'Singing for Fun'. Later in the same month the choir took part in a music festival.

Today this love of music is still strong in the school. The children learn to play musical instruments, they still take part in the music festival and there has even been a recent visit to the opera. The traditions of the past live on.

New Arrivals

Before a new child enters the school booklets are sent home to parents. These include a Home/School Agreement setting out clearly the aims of the school. These include offering 'a stimulating environment which will encourage academic, physical, social, moral and spiritual development.' A broad, balanced curriculum is offered with equal opportunities for every child. Parents are also advised on the contact that can be made between school and home so that parents are kept informed about the progress of their child.

When the agreement is signed the parent or guardian promises to send the child to school regularly and punctually, to observe the school uniform policy and support the school's behaviour guidelines. Perhaps most importantly they promise to help their child to do his/her best. The pupil too promises to attend school regularly and on time, wear tidy school uniform, bring equipment needed each day, do class and homework as well as possible, take care of the school site and look after school equipment and their own possessions.

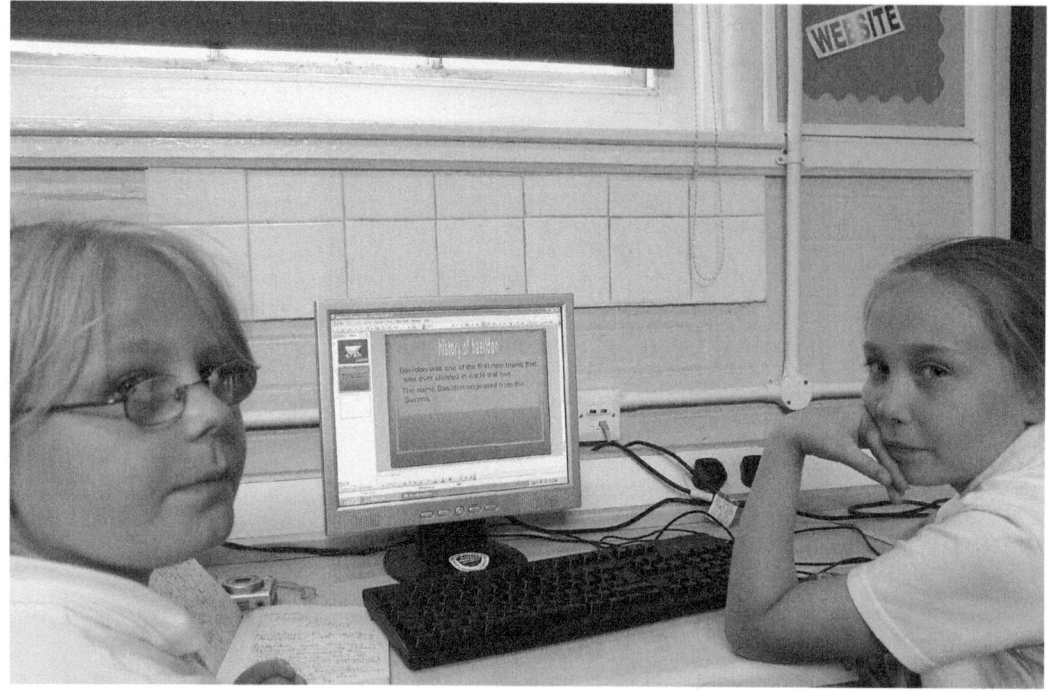

Working on the Basildon Heritage Project. (© Bob Fisher)

Discipline

'We do not control our children – they control themselves.' These words are to be found in the Pitsea Junior School booklet, sent to parents before their child joins the school. The headteacher and staff believe that a child's chance of success in school depends on his/her ability to make responsible choices. Parents and teachers, working together, can guide and support the children to make the right choices for themselves.

'We believe that Teaching and Learning are so important that no child can misbehave.' This approach of the school has three main parts – rules, rewards and sanctions. There are clear rules that each child can understand for behaviour around the school. Rewards help the child to follow the rules. Sanctions exist for those who break the rules and anyone who does so is well aware of the consequences that will follow. Remembering the school motto, pupils are advised to, 'Always set out to do your best. Do not be satisfied with anything less.'

Rewards

There are non-material rewards for good behaviour. This may simply be a smile, a nod or a word of encouragement. At other times children are sent to another member of staff for a special word of praise or the chance to be first to choose a book or game. Special jobs and responsibilities may also be given.

Out on the trail. (© Bob Fisher)

Stickers, certificates, stars of the day or week, house points and letters home are used as material rewards. There are also some more public rewards. Those who have maintained good behaviour and work for a week are able to join in Golden Time for thirty minutes. This is a time for fun. Those who have done well for a half term receive certificates in a special assembly and they may be given stamps, stickers, certificates and badges. There is a star of the week in each class and house points may also be given.

Sanctions

Occasionally things do go wrong. However, every child knows what will happen if rules are broken. It may not sound too bad to an adult, but to a primary school child the loss of time from Golden Time is very serious indeed. There is nothing worse than not being able to join in when the rest of your friends are having fun. There is a behaviour book in which bad behaviour can be recorded. Exclusion from school only happens in most extreme cases. There is no corporal punishment.

Looking Back

How very different it was in bygone days. Mrs Blant still has the old School Punishment Book. This records that caning, administered by the headteacher, was normal for any infringement of

A 1960s house. (Photographer Amy Skeggs, aged ten)

rules. In the 1920s this included up to four strokes on the hand for impertinence, bad behaviour, laziness, and using bad language in the vicinity of the school. One boy at this time was frequently sent to the headmaster. His misdemeanours included swearing, being a general nuisance in class, continual lateness and setting off a firework in the playground! Caning certainly didn't cure him of his anti-social behaviour.

The 1930s were also years when the cane was frequently used. One boy used a peashooter in class and then was unwise enough to be impertinent when taken to the headmaster. This resulted in a double punishment.

In the 1940s there was a case of five boys throwing pieces of coke, used at that time for heating the school. They ended up being mentioned in the Punishment Book and by the 1950s bad behaviour on a bus led to several boys appearing before the headteacher. This is something that would not have happened in earlier times when every child walked to school along unmade roads.

Photography

With the school shortly celebrating its centenary the headteacher has been delighted with the way the Heritage Project has helped to make the children more aware of their town. Photography was a completely new experience for the majority of the pupils and Bob Fisher's

The children who have taken part in the Heritage Project. (© Bob Fisher)

lesson helped them to see their surroundings in a different way. It has given them an awareness of the town and has guided them towards a greater understanding of their surroundings. Mrs Blant also commented on how excited the children were to have the sole use of high-tech cameras rather than having to share. The results of their work were impressive.

A School with a Past, Present and Future

Pitsea Junior School has almost completed its first 100 years. From its beginnings as a small village school it has grown to become a very important part of the community. Each year parents fill in a questionnaire and the results are increasingly positive. SATS results are steadily improving. Well over 70 per cent are around the national average. The majority of parents are very happy with the school and so are the majority of the children. The school is thriving and there seems little doubt that in the years to come the headteacher, staff and children will build on their present success.

9

St Anne Line Roman Catholic Junior

There Are No Strangers Here, Just Friends We Have Yet To Meet

These words are very important to the pupils and staff at St Anne Line School and as soon as you enter the front door you are greeted by friendly faces.

It was at 9.10 a.m. on a September day in 1964 that the new school first opened its doors. In those days it was known by the name of Blessed Anne Line. At that time there were 267 children on the roll, including 131 infants. Mr J. Fox was the first headmaster appointed.

That first morning was not without problems. No chairs had arrived. One can only imagine the frantic phone calls that must have been made before it was finally arranged for 300 to be borrowed from the church hall. Stationery too had not been delivered, but fortunately Woodlands School was able to help out. Then there were further problems at lunchtime with a shortage of tables in the dining hall, making the serving of those first-day meals a lengthy process.

Fortunately those early traumas are now long forgotten and there is a feeling of purposeful calm in the building today.

A Motto and a Badge

The school motto is *In Magna Constantia* (By Great Constancy). This motto has its roots in the early seventeenth century. Anne Line was a martyr and the words 'In great constancy' refer to the fact that she was constant in her faith and, even in the face of death, she refused to abandon her beliefs. Her story is told in pictorial form on one wall of the quadrangle. This mural was painted by the children with help from pupils at Woodlands School. It is now used to help to explain the main events in her life to new children joining the school. Her story is used as an example of someone with strongly held beliefs who stuck to her principles and realised that they were more important than anything else. The children learn that the principles of life are vital and they should never be compromised.

The school badge shows a key crossed with a feather. The key is there because Anne acted as a housekeeper to persecuted priests and the feather or palm is a symbol of martyrdom. Red, the colour of the school uniform, is also the colour of martyrdom.

The school noticeboard. (© Bob Fisher)

St Anne Line

The first thing you notice as your enter the school is the statue of St Anne Line, carved with a dove on her arm, the symbol of peace. When the school opened, her name was selected by the Bishop of Brentwood as she was one of the forty English Martyrs and had been born in Dunmow in Essex. The statue was given to the school by Mrs Magee and is hand carved from wood.

Anne was born into a Protestant family, probably in the late 1560s. Her father was a wealthy Calvinist who is believed to have lived with his family in the Clock House in Dunmow. At that time it was regarded as treason to be a Roman Catholic and the punishment could be imprisonment, exile or execution. Despite this Anne and her brother William converted to Catholicism. They were immediately disowned and disinherited by their father.

Anne was approximately nineteen years of age when she married Roger Line, another Roman Catholic convert. However, not long after the marriage Roger was arrested and exiled to Belgium, where he later died.

Left alone and in poverty, Anne became housekeeper to a group of priests living in London. In the latter days of the reign of Elizabeth I this was a dangerous occupation. However, she continued with her work, even when her adviser and friend, Father John Gerard, was captured

The statue of St Anne Line in the reception area of the school. (© Bob Fisher)

The St Anne Line Way on the wall of the school hall. (© Bob Fisher)

and imprisoned in the Tower of London. Then, on 2 February 1601, a large number of her fellow believers gathered for mass in her home. The authorities arrived; Anne was arrested and thrown into Newgate Prison. She was tried, found guilty of recusancy (refusal to attend Church of England services) and condemned to die on the scaffold at Tyburn. Here she knelt, on 27 February 1601, said her final prayers and was hanged. In 1929 she was beatified by Pope Pius XI, the first step to canonisation, and in 1970 her canonisation took place. The school still keeps her day and mass is celebrated as close as possible to 2 February each year, remembering her life and the day of her arrest.

A School in the Community

Nearly all of the Roman Catholic children from the parishes of St Therese and Holy Trinity are able to attend the school, although around 30 per cent of the pupils come from other denominations and faiths.

Martin Larrett became headmaster of St Anne Line in January 1989, following the retirement of Mr Fox, the first holder of the post. Martin has seen many changes in the years he has been leading the school and is extremely proud of its many achievements. In his own words:

> The school represents commitment to the community as well as aiming for high academic standards and good behaviour – in fact it offers all the things you would want from a school. The children involve themselves in a large number of outside activities so that their education is as broad as

possible. They should be outward looking and forward thinking. This is vital, as school is not simply about academic success. Children must be educated for their future lives. We have strong links with community activities in Basildon. We want our pupils to learn commitment in all they do and to realise that, although each person's contribution may be small, when joined with others we can really make a difference.

Playing the Game

Sport is very important at St Anne Line and teams have been delighted with their results over the years. Cricket, football, basketball, netball, cross-country running, swimming and athletics have all been enjoyed by pupils. In August, 2005, James Shane, a former pupil, won the first athletics gold medal at the European Youth Olympic Games in Italy at the age of fifteen. Some of those he beat were two years older. His record time of 3 mins 52.68 secs was nearly 4 seconds faster than his previous best set in the heats for 1,500m. This information is recorded on the 'Bygone Days' noticeboard. The present headmaster started the cricket team and one girl has been selected to play for the England Under-Fifteen team.

In various sports there have been excellent results, but sportsmanship is always emphasised as being more important than winning. Nevertheless, it is always exciting when a side does have success and this often happens. When the first Diocesan Cross-Country event was held in Hainault Forest it is proudly recalled that St Anne Line Juniors won the boys' and girls' races and also the overall team trophy! The football team has also had some outstanding results over the years.

Weather!

We sometimes think that our weather in the early years of the twenty-first century must be the worst ever recorded. However, the records show that this is not completely true. As other schools have mentioned, the January 1990 high winds were reminiscent of the great storms of 1987. Cladding was torn from the building, a window frame in one classroom suffered damage and the gate into the playground was torn from its hinges. Near neighbours lost fencing and even sheds but fortunately all the children reached home safely.

The following year, in February, the school opened in blizzard conditions. Only 140 pupils and four staff managed to attend. Two extra teachers from other schools reported to the school, presumably because they lived closer to St Anne Line than to their usual place of employment. Conditions became worse as the day went on. By midday it was decided to close the school and it remained shut the next day. Apparently over 8 inches of snow fell in twenty-four hours!

Rain also caused problems, especially for sports lessons. On 25 September 1992 a deluge of rain meant that 1 inch fell in just two hours and in November of the same year the playing field was badly flooded after almost continual rain for several weeks. In the spring of 1995 rain over a two-week period was 100 per cent greater than normal.

Outside the school building. (© Bob Fisher)

A Special Celebration

To mark the 400th anniversary of the death of St Anne Line the Bishop of Brentwood came to celebrate mass and the school's very own hymn about Anne Line was sung. The words had been written by one of the staff, Mrs Val Birch, some years previously and it has played a regular part in school assemblies ever since. Also, as part of the celebrations, a fountain was built in the very attractive quadrangle and this is another reminder of the life and death of the saint.

Shirley Butler

Mrs Shirley Butler joined the school in 1970 and she is now the office manager. Her own four children all attended the school and her second grandchild is also a pupil. She has seen many changes over the years but she still likes to call St Anne Line 'my school'. 'It is not like a place of work,' she says. 'The only cloud on the horizon is caused by the fact that, at some point, I will have to retire.' However, few people ever seem to sever all connections with the school, even many years after they have left.

The Quadrangle – an oasis of quiet in a busy school. (© Bob Fisher)

Children's Voices

Talking to some of the pupils was an interesting experience. Here are just a few of their comments:

'I like the teachers because they are all fun and they have a subject that they are really good at.' *Ceara Schoeman*

'I like the school because everyone is allowed to get involved and there's something special for everyone to do. We don't leave anyone out.' *Hannah Reid*

'What I like about this school are the teachers. They are cool and you treat them like people, not just teachers that you're scared of.' *Ravi Sharman*

'I like this school because it has lots to offer, not just lessons. There are lots of clubs and it's fun.' *Megan Patching*

'The thing I like about the school is the teachers, and the clubs that are going on, especially cricket.' *John Johnson*

'What I like about the school is that the teachers explain about things that will be useful later on in life and they explain them in a way that you can understand.' *Joseph Cassar*

'What I like is that everyone gets a fair chance for their opinion. They get a chance to say what clubs they would like to do and whether they would like to set up any clubs of their own.' *Charlotte Cavedasca*

'What I like about the school is that everyone shows respect, teachers and pupils, TAs [teaching assistants] and all the helpers. Also there is something for everyone to do, and there are Playground Friends. They help anyone who is being left out and I think that is very good.' *Lynsey Harradence*

Playground Friends

Playground Friends are elected at the beginning of the school year. They wear blue bibs so that they are easily identifiable and their role is to be there for anyone who feels lonely, needs someone to play with or has a problem and needs someone to listen. At playtime they are ready to lead games, help with drawing or just be there in case they are needed.

There is a rota so the 'Friends' can move around and help with different things on different days. Friendship Stops are set up. At one colouring may be offered, at another there is playground equipment and toys. The aim is to make sure that no one is left alone.

The children say it is fun being a Playground Friend because they are doing something they like and often people will come to them, not just because they are upset, but because these are people they like being with. Youngsters often find it easier to talk to another child about a problem like bullying, rather than saying anything more formally to an adult. The 'Friends' enjoy making up games and trying to ensure that they are as exciting as possible.

When children move into Year 3 each one has a Year 6 'Buddy'. This is someone the younger child can get to know well and if he or she has any problems the buddy will help to sort them out.

The playground. (© Bob Fisher)

A Day to Remember

A number of years ago one seven-year-old-pupil, Tommy, visited Shoeburyness. Whilst there he discovered a piece of metal on a bench. He thought this might be useful to include in the 'Moon' project his class was working on at school. Wondering if it could be opened he tried hitting it with a hammer, but it remained closed.

Tommy wrapped his prize in a towel and took it to school. It was then that the panic buttons began to ring. His teacher and the welfare assistant viewed the metal object with horror. The police were called and a bomb disposal unit rushed to the school. 560 children were evacuated from the building and stayed in the playground until lunchtime. When the experts arrived they decided that this was a highly dangerous unexploded bomb from the Second World War. Everyone who had been in contact with it had apparently been in a life-threatening situation. It was finally exploded in Gloucester Park.

Looking Back

In the week that the school first opened a representative called from a major supplier of biscuits. He was obviously hoping for a new customer. However, the headmaster informed him that supplies would not be required as there would be no tuck shop in the school. In January 1966 a dental inspection took place and Mr Fox recorded that the majority of children had teeth in good condition. He saw this as a vindication of his no-tuck-shop policy!

As the school numbers increased there was a need for extra classrooms. By 4 May 1966 land was being cleared, ready for building to start. Soon piles to support the foundations were drilled and, before the end of the month, the first bricks had been laid. Work continued well, although unsettled weather in June caused some problems. Yet by the end of the month the walls were 10ft high. School closed for the holidays in late July with high hopes that the new classrooms would be completely ready for the new term.

Alas, the school reopened in early September but the rooms were still unfinished and two classes had to be held in the church hall. Telephone calls were made to the architect. At the same time the playing field was not ready for use and the football pitch was not marked out, despite promises from the Education Department.

Fortunately, before the end of the month and following a number of letters and phone calls the pitch was marked and the two new classrooms were ready for use.

Two years later the infant school opened as a separate unit with its own headteacher.

Music

There are many accounts of the school taking part in concerts and music festivals. The children have sung at the Royal Albert Hall – a never-to-be-forgotten experience – and they took part in the Young Voices Concert held at the O2 Arena at the end of 2007. Peripatetic teachers visit the school to teach various musical instruments and there is a flourishing choir and an African drum group. The latter was formed after a group came to entertain the school

The frieze of St Anne Line's life painted on the Quadrangle wall. (© Bob Fisher)

with their drumming. Both the children and their teachers became enthusiastic about this type of music and a special project was organised to raise money to buy drums.

Under a government initiative every child in Years 4 and 5 is introduced to the flute. In fact enough flutes have been bought for the instrument to be taught in class groups. In May 1996 a music festival was held at the Towngate Theatre for the first time. According to the headmaster's report all the children sang well, but the show was stolen by the St Anne Line flute players, who entertained the audience with a full range of their playing ability and were a credit to the school.

Ofsted

Thoughts of inspections strike fear into the hearts of most teachers, however competent they are. In recent years the school has been inspected three times and on each occasion those fears have been proved to be ill-founded. It has been noted that the school's many strengths far outweigh any weaknesses. The more recent inspection was highly successful with the overall standard being assessed as good, but outstanding in moral, cultural and spiritual development, in terms of cultural diversity and in pastoral care.

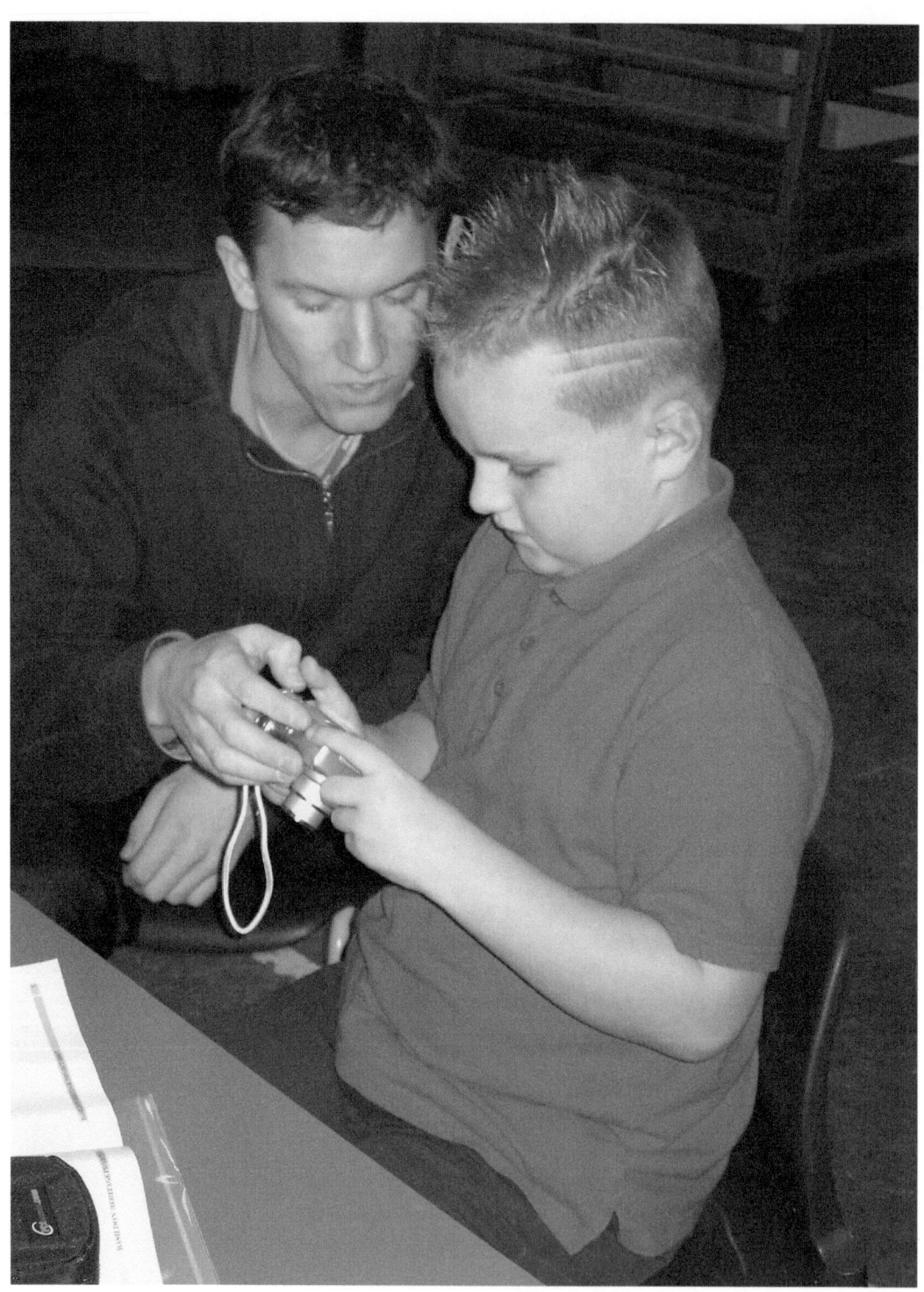

Teacher Paul Davis helping a young photographer. (© Bob Fisher)

Vin Harrop and young photographers at work on the trail. (© Bob Fisher)

The Heritage Project

Martin Larrett concluded that this was a great success as far as the school was concerned:

> The children were given the chance to explore the locality through an unusual route. The photographic slant was an excellent way to start off the project. This gave them the opportunity to look in a different way and to ask themselves what they were really looking at. Many modern children do not look enough. Looking, seeing and recognizing was something they had possibly never before taken on board. Also they learnt something about responsibility – what is valuable and what is not. If education has a real importance it is about developing that sort of understanding and how to be responsible for your own learning. By using the skills you have you can make a difference to other people as well.

The members of the Heritage Project Team certainly enjoyed working with all the children and their teacher, Mr Paul Davis. We hope that they have learnt new skills that will stay with them throughout their lives.

Year 5 class group. (© Bob Fisher)

The Past, the Present and the Future

St Anne Line School has now existed for over forty years. Many past pupils still keep in touch and for major events and celebrations they return and reunite, like members of a large family returning home. Two former pupils have gone on to become school captains at the Brentwood Ursuline School. Others proudly report back their sporting successes and other achievements. Many former pupils now have their own children in the school and this helps to make for a strong parent body giving support to the school. Traditions from the past are being built on and future generations will certainly benefit from the strengths that are now such an important part of the school life.

10

Looking Forward

A Changing Town

Most towns in Great Britain have evolved slowly over the centuries. Old buildings were often demolished as their space was needed in the name of progress. Today preservation orders are placed on structures that are deemed to have special significance so, in the future, there should be a mix of the new and the old.

As a New Town the Basildon we know today came into being in a very few years. It was created to deal with a post-war problem after numerous London houses had been destroyed during years of bombing. Following the compulsory purchase of many of the existing dwellings in Basildon it was time to make a completely fresh start. Land was cleared, architects employed and finally building started. Within a few years most of the homes, shops, offices and industrial sites were completed and the town flourished.

Although at first sight this must have seemed a great opportunity to create something completely new and to incorporate ideas that had not previously been used, it also led to problems. Over the years all the buildings have aged together. Many of the early buildings now look tired. Ideas on architecture have changed, as have the materials used in construction. What appeared modern in the 1950s and 1960s may no longer be acceptable.

The Basildon Renaissance Partnership

The District Council has decided to meet these problems head on. The Basildon Renaissance Partnership came into being in April 2002. Its function is to co-ordinate all Thames Gateway projects within the Basildon area. There are seven partners: Basildon District Council, The Department for Communities and Local Government, The East of England Development Agency, English Partnerships, Essex County Council, The Learning and Skills Council and Thames Gateway South Essex.

The redevelopment of the district will happen over the next fifteen to twenty years and there are five key priorities for regeneration. These are town-centre development, housing, the economy, culture and the environment and health education. Plans are already in operation and the biggest project in the district is the regeneration of Basildon town centre.

A pen-and-ink drawing of Basildon by Ronald Maddox, 1965. (Reproduced by kind permission of the Basildon Arts Trust)

This will be one of the largest town redevelopments in the country. There will be new homes, new shops, new facilities, new restaurants, new office space, a new railway station and transport hub.

The Railway Station Area
So what will this mean for the people of Basildon?

Firstly, if all the plans are approved, the railway station will be moved a short way to the west. The present structure is thought to be too small for the ever-expanding community. This new station, it is hoped, will be an impressive gateway to the town. It will have cafés and shops that offer a real welcome to visitors.

Not only will the station building change, but the whole area to the north will also alter. The present market will move to become a street market in the area leading down from St Martin's Square. Stalls will be stored on non-market days, leaving the road clear for pedestrians. The old market will then become the station square.

In the new station area it is also proposed to build the Town Hall, making this the administrative centre of the town. This is also where the theatre and library will be situated. Some hope that a museum and an art gallery may also be included.

It is suggested that there will be an improved bus hub area. A series of high-quality bus stops will be built along Southernhay.

The Town Centre

With a new Town Hall and theatre being planned, what will happen to the existing buildings? It is envisaged that these will be demolished and a green link developed from Gloucester Park to St Martin's Square. This will include an extension to the lake, bringing it right into the town centre. Obviously it is unusual to have a large park so close to the centre of a town and it is believed that these changes will make the park and town even more accessible to each other.

A big change to this area is the proposal to build new homes with private gardens and a formal garden linking the park and the town centre. Previously the only homes in the centre of the town have been the apartments in Brooke House. It is thought there will be more than 3,000 people dwelling in the central area when the changes are complete. Alterations will have to be made to the traffic flow in Broadmayne.

The gardens in St Martin's Square should remain with the church and bell tower forming interesting features to the north of the square. Possibly the green area in front of the church will be extended and there could be cafés, bars or restaurants in the corner of the square.

The Town Square

The town square, with its huge open space in the centre, will remain largely as it is, but there will be some improvements. The old escalator has already been demolished and this will be replaced by a glass lift and extra seating will be provided in the square itself. Brooke House dominates the skyline of Basildon and also the square, appearing to float on its interesting columns. Designed by Sir Basil Spence, this is a listed building and, although it may well be refurbished, it should remain.

Two glass pavilions stand in the square at the moment: one is a Costa Coffee café where customers may sit outside in bright weather under colourful umbrellas, the other is Toni & Guy, the hairdressers. A third pavilion is also envisaged. It is hoped to encourage more leisure activities in the area so that it will become a meeting point into the evening.

Special features, like the Mother and Child statue and the round clock, should stay in place.

The Eastgate Centre

The Eastgate Centre is already being refurbished. This will be a focal point for high-quality shopping. It is hoped that, in the future, there may be pedestrian access through the centre out of shopping hours, making easier access to the main town centre. It is hoped that this will lead to greater integration of Eastgate with the rest of the town.

Basildon's Sporting Village

A very exciting proposal for the development of Basildon is the Sporting Village. Some worry about the encroachment into the open space. Gloucester Park has always been considered as one of the most inspired ideas of the early developers of the New Town. This beautiful green lung, with its manmade hills, tranquil lake, superb trees and sports facilities has been a real gem in the town's crown. However, with the new suggestions for the town centre, it should become even more accessible to the whole population.

There are some structural problems with the existing swimming pool and it has now been decided to create a completely new sports complex in the north-western corner of Gloucester Park. This will be developed beside the existing athletics track and close to the sports pitches. The vision is to have a landmark building with recreational facilities suitable not just for local needs but also of a standard acceptable for regional and national competitions.

Part of the plan is to include an Olympic-sized 50m swimming pool with eight lanes that can also be split into two 25m community pools. There will also be a gymnastic centre that is planned to be the home of South Essex Gymnastics Club. Funding is now in place with government endorsement and £5 million granted towards the £34 million estimated to be needed for the whole project. Basildon District Council and Essex County Council have pledged £20 million for the scheme. It is hoped to raise the extra money required from sports funding bodies and the private sector.

As part of the indoor facilities an eight-court multi-purpose sports hall will be built and a health and fitness gymnasium.

The Vision

The planners believe that the Sporting Village will bring new unity to the town and help to build a better community spirit. It is hoped that schools, local hospitals, businesses and the Primary Care Trusts will all be enthusiastic about this new development. At a time when there are considerable worries about obesity, good sports facilities should play their part in keeping our local people healthy.

So why was Gloucester Park chosen as the best location for the Village? There are a number of answers. It is well connected to local transport and is close to the town centre where many people will work and live. Also it is central to other sporting activities. There is room for further expansion if needed and this is the one place in the town where both indoor and outdoor sports can take place alongside each other. Outside, apart from the athletics track, there will be a grandstand, a synthetic pitch, netball courts and rugby, cricket and football pitches.

Other ideas being considered include an area for indoor bowls, a climbing wall, leisure and learner water, a soft play area and squash courts. The aim is to have the centre open in 2010. Being so close to London and with the 2012 Olympic Games drawing ever closer this promises to be a superb facility for the town and the whole area. It could also be used as a training camp for nations competing in the Olympic and Paralympic Games.

The Master Plan

Although the main concentration in this book has been on the centre of Basildon there are plans for improvements to all the town centres covered by Basildon District Council. These will be rather lower key than the changes in Basildon town centre, but the plans will nevertheless be comprehensive. In all these plans much thought will be given to the inclusion of public space, gardens and arts projects and improving the quality of life for the people of the district.

Working for the Basildon Renaissance Partnership

Those working for the Basildon Renaissance Partnership are extremely enthusiastic about the project and this comes through when they talk about the future of the town. As one officer interviewed said:

> This is an exciting time for the district. You have to move with the times, without neglecting the history of the place. Basildon is part of the Thames Gateway and this is a once in a lifetime opportunity to coordinate these plans and make sure that they are done in the right way for the community. There is a lot of private interest in Basildon in terms of investment, with companies putting their money into the district. It is important that this is coordinated by engaging the public and making sure that Basildon gets the best for its people both now and for the future.

Basildon Hospital

Basildon hospital became a world-class cardiothoracic centre in July 2007. This was when the new £60 million centre opened its doors to patients. It offers specialist diagnosis and treatment for those with heart and lung diseases and the treatment is second to none. There are state-of-the art operating theatres and laboratories and facilities for 100 patients. This is a remarkable addition to the services already being offered by the hospital. In the past there have been problems with very limited parking space, but plans are in hand to offer better transport accommodation in the future.

Towards Tomorrow

In this book we have looked at Basildon's past, which is so often forgotten. The town does have an interesting and unique history. From early times small communities have chosen to live and settle in this area. More recently there have been the plotlanders, many of whom came from war-torn London and faced very difficult conditions, without any of the normal services we take for granted in the twenty-first century. Later new arrivals made their homes on what was at first a giant building site. There were promises that things would be better in the future, but day-to-day living was hard. However, the majority stayed and, over the years, made their own contribution to the life of the town.

We have also looked at the present and the establishment of a Lottery-funded Heritage Trail. Five local schools have been very much involved in walking the trail for the first time and finding out more about places of interest in the town. Each of those schools has a unique and very special history of their own and the children are making a real contribution to the future of their town.

Lastly we have turned to the future. The Renaissance Partnership has great plans for the development of Basildon. Local history books often stay on bookshelves and in libraries for many years. Some readers of *Basildon, Our Heritage* will know how many of the ideas were changed, altered or adopted. Whatever happens one thing is certain – Basildon is a town of which we can all be justly proud. It is truly our town and our heritage.

An abstract sculpture with Brooke House beyond taken from Basildon Arts Centre, 1969. (© Vin Harrop)

Bibliography

A Century of Basildon, Marion Hill, Sutton Publishing
Basildon, Peter Lucas, Phillimore & Co. Ltd
Basildon: A History & Celebration, Mara Cottrell, Francis Frith Collection
Basildon: A Pictorial History, Jessie K. Payne, Phillimore & Co. Ltd
Basildon: A Quiz & Miscellany, Mara Cottrell, Francis Frith Collection
Basildon in Old Photographs, Marion Hill, Sutton Publishing
Basildon Plotlands, Deanna Walker, Phillimore & Co. Ltd
History of Basildon, Billericay & Wickford, Basildon Council
Memories of Basildon, Jim Reeve, Tempus Publishing Ltd
Plotland Memories, Karen McKay, Essex Wildlife Trust
When Basildon was Farms & Fields, Jessie K. Payne, Ian Henry Publications

Other local titles published by The History Press

Gravesham
JOHN GUY

Illustrated with around 150 old photographs, this book presents a complete historical picture of the region including a chapter on the outlying villages that make up the borough of Gravesham. All the pictures illustrating the historical theme of each chapter have been taken exclusively from the Gravesham Library collection and, combined with a substantial collection of contemporary views, provide an interesting insight into Gravesham's past.

978 07524 4257 0

Memories of Basildon
JIM REEVE

Modern Basildon has its roots in the railways and the decision of The Land Co. in 1891 to buy up land from cash-strapped farmers and sell it on in plots. In this book the children of these original plotlanders vividly recall their experiences: how they lived, went to school and played, along with more modern reminiscences of the schooldays, wartime and working life of the newcomers who arrived in the New Town from London and all parts of the country.

978 07524 3819 1

The Billericay School
SYLVIA KENT

The creation of the Billericay School in 1937 as the town's first senior school marked the beginning of an exciting new era for the town and its families. This collection of over 200 photographs presents a unique pictorial record of the history of the school and its forerunner, the Great Burstead Board School. This book chronicles some of the changes and events for all those involved: teachers, parents, and pupils.

978 07524 3083 6

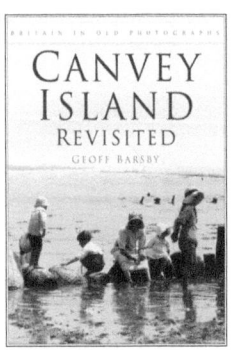

Canvey Island Revisited
GEOFF BARSBY

Following on from the first two collections of archive images, this new volume revisits the Canvey Island of yesteryear with the use of 200 fascinating photographs, postcards and other ephemera. As well as demonstrating the diversity of islanders throughout history. *Canvey Island Revisited* is an important pictorial history that will be of interest to all those who have ever lived in the area.

978 07524 3984 6

If you are interested in purchasing other books published by The History Press, or in case you have difficulty finding any History Press books in your local bookshop, you can also place orders directly through our website

www.thehistorypress.co.uk